Successful Farming
—*By Phone*

Steve Kennedy

Calculated Industries, Inc.
2010 North Tustin • Orange • California • 92665

Also by Steve Kennedy

Successful Farming—By Mail
How to Get the Most fromYour Financial I™

Special thanks to Debbie Johnson and Constance Smith.

Publication Data

Kennedy, Steve C., 1957–
  Successful farming by phone.

  (Real estate for professional practitioners)
  Includes index.

  ISBN 0-944041-02-7

Printed in the United States of America.

Table of Contents

*To my Mother and Father, who
made it all possible.
Thanks.*

1. Introduction to Farming By Phone

Back in the 1800s, a man could stake out a piece of land, cut and clear away the brush, plow it to harvest, and within a period of time, legally claim it as his own.

The days of land giveaways are gone forever, but it's still true that working a piece of territory can pay off handsomely — if we set our stakes around carefully chosen groups of people.

The top salespeople of our time know that singling out a section of the market and making it the focus of their selling strategy is the key to success.

That's one of Lee Iacocca's secrets. Early on, he recognized that dealers are really the only customers a car company has. So he went out of his way to keep them happy.

In real estate, your *potential* market is much, much bigger. And that makes narrowing your efforts, or *farming* a specific group, all the more important.

In short, farming lets you turn "hit-or-miss" income into a steady stream of commission checks.

What Is a Farm?

As a real estate professional, your *farm* (or *listing farm)* is a select group of prospects you claim as yours to cultivate. From that moment on, you concentrate much of your energy and time on trying to produce listings and potential buyers (either directly or through referrals) from the people who make it up.

A farm can be either: (1) *territorial* — a certain geographic section of your city or town, or (2) *social* — a particular group, perhaps geographically separate but belonging to the same organization or club.

Whatever the specifics, your farm is territory from which you can reap rich rewards, if you plow and sow as faithfully and lovingly as our great-grandfathers did their land.

How Farming Works

Unlike the stockbroker or insurance agent, the real estate salesperson lacks continual contact with his or her clients. When the stockbroker gets a hot tip, he or she has a Rolodex full of prospects to call. And the insurance agent has it even better. Even without any direct contact, he or she gets renewals (and renewal commissions) each year.

Unfortunately, in real estate there are typically no hot tips, no automatic renewals. Worst of all, even your best and most satisfied clients may not be heard from for many, many years.

Building and nurturing a continuing relationship with a set number of prospects or clients is what real estate farming is all about.

And more than anything else, this requires a

tremendous amount of careful communication.

And in communicating with your farm, you have a choice of methods. For each, the variations are limited only by your imagination. But in essence, the people who live in your farm come to know you in one of three ways: (1) through personal, face-to-face visits, (2) through phone calls, and (3) through letters and other mailings such as newsletters.

Each method has its advantages and for maximum impact, of course, all three work together.

Here's a good example of how the three together can help you:

In the monthly newsletter he mails to his farm, Agent Ralph Smith writes a few catchy descriptions of new listings in the area.

Within a day or two, one of the 250 prospects who received the newsletter calls Ralph for more information. Now renting, she's interested in owning a home.

Over the phone, Ralph finds out the kind of home she's looking for, the price range, the size of her family, and what special features interest her most.

The next evening, Ralph is at her apartment, with descriptions of five or six homes that fit her needs. He begins showing her homes and, within a few weeks, he writes up an offer. The deal goes through.

Unfortunately, it's rarely that simple, but without communication there would be no sale. Moreover, all too often we overlook the critical importance of every step in the communication process.

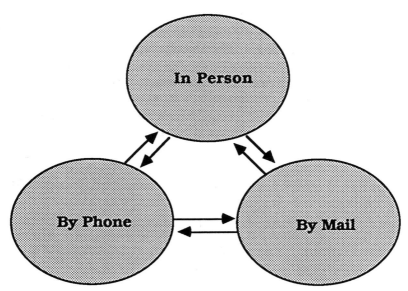

The three main ways to communicate with your farm are in person, by phone, and by mail. Ideally, all three work together.

But the little impressions we leave along the way are what cement the relationship between an agent and a client. And paying attention to them pays off.

About This Book

In this book, you're going to look primarily at how to handle communication with your farm over the telephone.

We'll start off with a brief overview of tele-marketing — the '80s term for telephone sales — and then move to a step-by-step analysis of what's undoubtedly one of the biggest hurdles for most of us: making cold calls to your farm.

Later, you'll look at what to do when your phone

rings, with tips on how to turn a caller into a client.

And finally, you'll put it all together with some odds and ends to give you a cohesive plan of attack for your telephone farming.

Remember all the while that it takes all three kinds of communication — letters, phone calls, and face-to-face visits — to make a farm work. (In fact, some studies show that following up a letter with a phone call can generate 10 times the response of a letter alone.)

If you're an old hand at farming by phone, this book may have a few tips that could help increase your harvest. If farming is new to you, this book will not only help you develop the right techniques, it should also help give you the confidence you need to succeed in all areas of telephone sales.

There are certain truths that all of us know but need to be reminded of. One of them is that sales is really a matter of helping people get what they want. In other words, we're not simply selling houses and getting listings; we're helping people own the homes of their dreams.

And in those words lies a world of difference.

2. Staking Out Your Farm

Probably three fourths of all real estate agents operate their businesses the way they do their lives: randomly, reacting to whatever comes along. But successful agents don't merely react, they initiate.

Remember the old sales adage: "Plan your work and work your plan."

For the real estate professional in today's competitive environment, a key element in that plan must be selecting a farm.

Looking for Virgin Territory

Before you settle on where you're going to stake your claim, keep a few things in mind.

For example, do you enjoy walking through a neighborhood, chatting with people on their front porches? Or do you prefer the higher energy of social gatherings?

One well-known life insurance agent sets up weekly luncheons with prospective clients at fine hotels. Superficially, it doesn't seem that much business is discussed. But he cultivates his clients carefully and he's so well liked, he writes up millions of dollars' worth of policies every year.

For those of us without his superb social graces, it's probably easiest to specialize in particular neighborhoods.

But before you make a decision, drive around the area. See how many other realtors have listings there. If you spot a number of different signs, that means that most likely no single agent has yet been able to establish his or her claim.

But if all you see are the signs of one realtor, it's probably best to back off. There are plenty of other spots ripe for the picking.

The same considerations operate when you're choosing a club or social group to compose your farm. Chances are one or two other realtors may have had the same idea. But they won't be as easy to spot as the *for sale* signs in the front yard. So move ahead with care. And don't make a commitment until you're sure the ground is ready.

Checking Out the Territory

Before moving in on your farm, make sure you do your homework. Certain practical considerations are important.

The People Who Live There

The first, of course, is the kind of people who live there. Are they people you can relate to easily? Would you feel comfortable in that kind of environment yourself? Do you think you share similar interests and concerns?

Income Potential of the Territory

Second, look at the income potential from your farm. Go through records to see what homes in that area have sold for over the past year or so. (Most title insurance companies will be able to assist you with this, by the way.)

Figure out what your potential commissions could run. Assume that if you farm your market well, in time you could capture 40% to 60% (maybe 75%) of the listings. How much income would that be for you each year?

The Optimal Size Farm

Third, consider what size farm you feel you could effectively manage. Higher-priced homes require more effort in marketing, so 200 may be your limit. If it's a neighborhood of tract homes, perhaps you could handle 500. Be realistic. Don't let potential profits lure you into trying to run a farm that's too big to handle properly.

Let Commissions Be Your Guide

For most people, the best method for sizing up a farm is based on your specific income goals and the commissions needed to reach them.

To begin, you must establish in your own mind a reasonable and attainable goal of how much money you want to generate *from your farm* in gross commissions. Remember, of course, you will still have other revenue sources outside of your farm.

To find out what size farm you need to attain your commission goal — which for this example we'll assume to be $45,000 per year — you will need to look at several ratios. So grab a pencil, some scratch paper, and your calculator. The ratios to look at are:

1. *Average Gross Commission Percentage*
2. *Average Sales Price*
3. *Average Gross Commission Dollars*
4. *Annual Turnover Rate*
5. *Farm Penetration Percentage (estimated)*

Average Gross Commission Percentage — This one is a little tricky. It pertains to the number of homes on which you will split a commission (via co-op sales) versus the number of homes you sell on your own and for which you will keep the full commission.

For this ratio it is best to use your own past listing history. For example, say last year you had 40 listings, and of those, 30 were sold through cooperative multiple listings (50/50 split between the listing agent and selling agent), and the other 10 were sold outright. If 6% is the normal commission in your area, then that means you had an overall Average Gross Commission Percentage per listing as follows:

```
30 Listings x .03 (3%) Ea. =  .90
10 Listings x .06 (6%) Ea. =  .60
                           = 1.50 ÷ 40 Listings = .0375 (3.75%)
```

This means the Average Gross Commission on each of your listings was 3.75%.

Average Sales Price — This is fairly straight-forward. You simply find the average sales price for homes sold in the prospective farm area. Add all of the sales prices together and divide by the number of homes sold. For simplicity, say those 40 homes sold for a total of $4,800,000.

$4,800,000 ÷ 40 Homes = $120,000 Average Sales Price

Average Gross Commission Dollars — Here you simply take the Gross Commission Percentage calculated above and multiply it by the Average Sales Price.

In this case, that is $120,000 x 3.75%, or $4,500, which means you will generate $4,500 in gross commission dollars for each listing you get.

So with this calculated, you can now find the number of listings you need to obtain in order to reach your goal of $45,000 in gross commissions:

$45,000 ÷ $4,500 per Listing = 10 Listings Needed

Now that you have determined the number of listings required, you need just two more pieces of information: the area's Annual Turnover Rate and your Farm Penetration.

Annual Turnover Rate — This is the "formula" for determining the number of homes sold in any given year, typically the most recent year, in your prospective farm area. Or it can be calculated from your board or multiple listing service (MLS) information.

Basically the formula works like this: Divide the total number of sales for the year by the size of the prospective farm.

# Homes Sold in Last 12 Months	68
÷ Total Size of Prospective Farm	÷ 580
Annual Turnover Rate	11.72%

So you know that for the example problem, you have an Annual Turnover Rate of 11.72%.

(To get a more accurate figure, it is often best to take a couple of years' worth of information. If you do this, make sure you use the *yearly average* for your calculation.)

If you divide the number of listings needed to meet the income goal (from above) by the Annual Turnover Rate, you get the total farm size. This assumes that you got *all* of the listings in the farm.

10 Listings ÷ 11.72% Turnover Rate = 85.32 (or 85) Homes

But you are not quite finished yet. Nobody gets all of the listings in a farm area — even the best farmers get nudged out by relatives, etc.

That is where the final ratio, Farm Penetration, comes into play.

Farm Penetration — This is the percentage of total homes listed in the farm area on which you will get the listing. Obviously this will vary — 40% is very good, and 50% to 65% is outstanding.

Just starting out, you cannot expect to harvest the same results as if you had been working at it for awhile. Moreover, it is going to take time, usually 6 to 18 months, just to get it started.

For the example here (one in which you are starting a brand new farm) use 35% Farm Penetration.

Now that you have estimated the Farm Penetration, all you need to do is divide the number of homes needed, if you got *all* the listings in the farm, by the Farm Penetration to get your necessary farm size.

85 Homes ÷ 35% Penetration = 242.86 (or 243) Homes

At last, you have done it! Summarizing, in order to achieve gross commissions of $45,000 from your farm, you must have a farm size of 243 homes. This is based on an Average Sales Price of $120,000, a 11.72% Turnover Rate, your ability to get 35% of the listings in the farm (35% Farm Penetration), and your ability to sell one fourth of the farm listings outright and the other three fourths through your co-op multiple listing service.

The completed "Prospective Farm Size" work-sheet on the next page, and the blank one on the two pages that follow, are designed to help you determine your optimal farm size based on your own income goals.

Prospective Farm Size
— Example

Your Annual Commission Goal $45,000

1. Average Gross Comm. Percentage
- # 30 Co-Op Listings   x 3 %   = .90
- # 10 Solo Listings   x 6 %   = .60

   Sum 40   Total % = 1.50
   Divide Total % by # of listings   ÷ 40
   Average Gross Commision % = 3.75%

2. Average Sales Price
- Add up all sales prices for farm area and div. by the # of homes sold = $120,000

3. Average Gross Comm. Dollars
- Multiply Avg. Sale Price (#2) $120,000
  by Avg. Gross Comm. % (#1)   x   3.75%
  Avg. Gross Comm. Dollars = $ 4,500

4. Number of Listings Needed
- Divide Annual Comm. Goal   45,000
  by Avg. Comm. Dollars (#3)   ÷ $4,500
  Number of Listings Needed = 10

5. Annual Turnover Rate
- Divide number of sales for year   68
  by total number of homes in prospective farm (or MLS) area   ÷ 580
  Annual Turnover Rate = 11.72%

6. Farm Size If You Got 100% of Listings
- Divide Number of Listings (#4)   10
  by Ann. Turnover Rate (#5)   ÷ 11.72%
  Farm Size at 100% of Listings = 85

7. Farm Penetration
- Est. percentage of homes in the farm
  on which you'll get the listing   = 35%

8. Final Size of Farm Needed for Goal
- Divide Farm Size at 100% (#6)   85
  by Farm Penetration (#7)   ÷ 35%

   Actual Size of Farm Needed = 243

Example of completed Prospective Farm Size sheet.

Sizing Up Your Farm

Prospective Farm #1

Your Annual Commission Goal $ _____

1. **Average Gross Comm. Percentage**
   - # _____ Co-Op Listings   x _____ % = _____
   - # _____ Solo Listings   x _____ % = _____
   - Sum _____ Total % = _____
     Divide Total % by # of listings _____ ÷ _____
     Average Gross Commision % = _____ %

2. **Average Sales Price**
   - Add up all sales prices for farm area and divide by the # of homes sold   = $ _____

3. **Average Gross Comm. Dollars**
   - Multiply Avg. Sale Price (#2) _____
     by Avg. Gross Comm. % (#1) _____ x _____
     Avg. Gross Comm. Dollars = $ _____

4. **Number of Listings Needed**
   - Divide Annual Comm. Goal _____
     by Avg. Comm. Dollars (#3) _____ ÷ _____
     Number of Listings Needed = _____

Prospective Farm #2

Your Annual Commision Goal $ _____

1. **Average Gross Comm. Percentage**
   - # _____ Co-Op Listings   x _____ % = _____
   - # _____ Solo Listings   x _____ % = _____
   - Sum _____ Total % = _____
     Divide Total % by # of listings _____ ÷ _____
     Average Gross Commision % = _____ %

2. **Average Sales Price**
   - Add up all sales prices for farm area and divide by the # of homes sold   = $ _____

3. **Average Gross Comm. Dollars**
   - Multiply Avg. Sale Price (#2) _____
     by Avg. Gross Comm. % (#1) _____ x _____
     Avg. Gross Comm. Dollars = $ _____

4. **Number of Listings Needed**
   - Divide Annual Comm. Goal _____
     by Avg. Comm. Dollars (#3) _____ ÷ _____
     Number of Listings Needed = _____

5. **Annual Turnover Rate**
    - Divide number of sales for year by total number of homes in prospective farm (or MLS) area

    _____ ÷ _____ = _____ %
    Annual Turnover Rate

6. **Farm Size If You Got 100% of Listings**
    - Divide Number of Listings (#4) by Ann. Turnover Rate (#5)
    Farm Size at 100% of Listings

    _____ ÷ _____ = _____

7. **Farm Penetration**
    - Est. percentage of homes in the farm on which you'll get the listing

    _____ = _____ %

8. **Final Size of Farm Needed for Goal**
    - Divide Farm Size at 100% (#6) by Farm Penetration (#7)

    _____ ÷ _____ = _____
    Actual Size of Farm Needed

5. **Annual Turnover Rate**
    - Divide number of sales for year by total number of homes in prospective farm (or MLS) area

    _____ ÷ _____ = _____ %
    Annual Turnover Rate

6. **Farm Size If You Got 100% of Listings**
    - Divide Number of Listings (#4) by Ann. Turnover Rate (#5)
    Farm Size at 100% of Listings

    _____ ÷ _____ = _____

7. **Farm Penetration**
    - Est. percentage of homes in the farm on which you'll get the listing

    _____ = _____ %

8. **Final Size of Farm Needed for Goal**
    - Divide Farm Size at 100% (#6) by Farm Penetration (#7)

    _____ ÷ _____ = _____
    Actual Size of Farm Needed

This form is designed to help you determine the size of your farm or to compare a couple of farms.

Setting Your Boundaries

You may choose to have several small farms scattered across the city, each one representing a different type of home or income level. Or, you may channel your efforts into one particular condominium or housing development, or targeted geographical area.

Either route can prove profitable. Both have their advantages and disadvantages.

Having several small farms gives you the edge of diversification — i.e., not putting all your eggs in the same basket. This might be a good way to test the waters if you're just starting out in real estate or in real estate farming.

Selecting a homogeneous farm, however, is probably better in the long run as it allows you to better pinpoint your selling efforts. It's hard to be all things to all people.

But either way you go, cultivate your farm with care.

At any moment, another real estate agent may try to take over your territory. And since most of us can't offer price breaks, special discounts, or other traditional short-term marketing incentives, the only edge we have is the time and effort we spend working our farms — and the relationships we develop from them.

If the people who live in your farm see you as a genuinely caring person, sincerely interested in them and their families, don't sweat over the competition. It'll be almost impossible to break the trust people have placed in you.

Final Considerations

Whether you choose a territorial or social farm, it's up to you. Use whatever works best. But don't let your ambition exceed your abilities. If a farm has 1,000 homes or names, to personally visit each one twice a year, you'd have to see eight people every day, five days a week, 50 weeks a year. You'd have no time left for anything else.

On the other hand, mailing to 1,000 homes would be simple and relatively inexpensive, considering the discount the US Postal Service grants on bulk mailings of 200 pieces or more.

Remember, the key to farming is balancing mail, phone calls, and personal visits for maximum impact. So you must consider the ramifications of all three when you select your farm.

Other Farm Benefits

One of the biggest advantages of a farm is that you have the opportunity to make friends with literally hundreds of people. You enjoy all the benefits of warm and caring relationships, knowing that when it's time to move, you'll be the first one they call to help them find or sell a home.

Years ago, when I decided to buy my first home (prior to getting into the real estate business myself), I called or visited with probably 20 real estate agents. One stood out from all the rest.

I had stopped by her office for five minutes in November. Two months later, I called. Right away, she remembered that I had been there with my brother. That kind of personal attention kept me with her through a house deal that was stitched together with the thinnest of thread.

Finally, your farm isn't a collection of houses or a list of names. It's people. If you take care of them, they'll take care of you.

Summary

In this chapter you nailed down some of the basics of selecting a farm. The ideal selection process begins with a goal-oriented approach based on your specific income (commission) desires.

Then, you can refine the type of farm you want by asking yourself the following questions:

> *Do you prefer to work a particular territory, or is a social group more to your liking?*
>
> *Once you've picked a neighborhood or organization, can you feel comfortable relating to it?*
>
> *Check out the sales records for the area you're considering. What's the average selling price of the homes?*
>
> *What's the average turnover rate?*
>
> *Is there enough potential commission to be earned?*
>
> *Don't for to see what your competition is doing. Does it look like someone has already staked out the territory, or is it wide open?*

Finally, head for your farm, thinking of it not only as a way for you to become financially secure, but also as a means of helping people answer questions about what is probably their most treasured asset, their home.

3. Telemarketing: Wave of the Future

Today the average face-to-face sales call in this country costs more than $200. On the other hand, the price of the average telephone sales call is about $3.50.

More and more businesses are catching on to the fact that using the phone can save time and money. After all, while the cost of almost everything else keeps rising, phone rates — thanks to deregulation and the increased competition it brought on — are actually decreasing.

And that's good news for almost everyone in sales.

What Is Telemarketing?

Basically, telemarketing means using the phone to help make sales. It's a new word for an old-fashioned concept, but it's appropriate when you consider the changes in our society.

When Jackie Bouvier married into the Kennedy family, she had to get used to the ease with which they picked up the phone to make long-distance calls.

In her family, a long-distance call meant something special. To the Kennedys, it was routine.

The way we think about telephones has changed a lot over the past 10 years. We have wireless phones we can take outside, cellular phones in our cars, and Mickey Mouse phones for our children — more and more, the telephone is a part of everyday life.

For businesses, telemarketing began to take off during the energy crunch of the '70s. That's when companies really began looking for alternatives to personal sales calls — and the gas-guzzling cars it took to make them.

After all, it costs a lot of money to keep a salesperson in the field — with cars, hotel bills, meal expenses, lots of time in waiting rooms, missed appointments, and delays in getting the orders back to the office.

Moreover, the average outside sales rep spends less than a third of his or her time actually selling.

Many companies found that regularly scheduled phone calls to small towns or isolated customers worked just as well or better in keeping up with orders. They also began using the phone to call former customers, politely asking why they no longer used their business.

Sales Expenses:

Face-to-Face Sales Call
Salesperson's time
Automobile
Meals
Missed appointment time
Hotels
Misc. (parking, tolls, etc.)

Telephone Sales Call
Salesperson's time (minimal)
Phone charges

Sales Time:

Face-to-Face Sales Call		*Telephone Sales Call*	
Drive to appt.	.50 hr.	Dial number	10 sec.
Waiting	.25 hr.		
Drive from appt.	.50 hr.		

For many, telemarketing resulted not only in dramatic decreases in the cost of sales, but in increased sales as well. As a result, outside sales forces were scaled down, phone lines were installed, and inside, telephone sales staffs were increased — and the telemarketing boom was born . Today companies are using telemarketing to:

- *Strengthen their marketing mix*
- *Search for prospective customers*
- *Expand markets*
- *Reach distant or marginal customers*
- *Beef up direct-mail campaigns*
- *Get appointments for salesmen*

And it is used to sell everything from grapefruits to fine art, to life insurance, and high tech industrial products — almost anything you can think of.

Obviously, your chances of wrapping up a real estate deal on the phone are remote. But at every step along the way, Alexander Graham Bell's brainchild can save you time and money.

Why Is Telemarketing Growing?

Sales experts nationwide agree that *telemarketing* — or using the telephone as a sales tool — is the "wave of the future." Moreover, it's the fastest growing sales tool of the '80s.

According to the Direct Marketing Association, telemarketing is a $100 billion-a-year business, with revenues jumping about 30% a year.

It already plays an important part in the strategies of 80,000 US companies, and within the next few years, that number should skyrocket to more than 265,000 firms.

Our world today moves at a faster pace. We have overnight courier services, computer modems, fast foods you buy at a drive-up window, and instant food you pop into your microwave.

Decisions are made faster, products sold more quickly, and credit extended more readily. Dramatic evidence of this change of pace is seen in the phenomenal growth of the direct-mail catalog industry.

Where once Sears and Montgomery Ward dominated the market, now there's a veritable cornucopia of catalogs, targeted at everyone from the luxury consumer to science buffs to the disabled.

And if you're really in a hurry — which most of are — almost all of them have toll-free "800" numbers for you to call and charge your order to your credit card. Many of them are staffed 24 hours a day.

Face it. We're getting used to buying and selling with our fingertips.

Add in the increased number of two-wage-earner families and the growing mobility of Americans, and it's easy to see why the phone has replaced the mail as our primary means of communicating.

Advantages of Telemarketing

If you're looking at dollars and cents, from a business standpoint, selling by phone makes a lot of sense. Using the phone can save you time and money. But there are many other advantages as well.

Projects a Positive Image

When you dial a number on a sales call, your prospect is one step removed from you. That means he or she feels less pressure because over the phone, it's easier to say no than face-to-face. Also, calling first lifts you out of the door-to-door salesperson category and, if you use the right approach, can give you an increased aura of professionalism.

Eliminates a Bad First Impression

Some authorities claim that what we say is only 7% of our message. The way we say it is 38% and our body language or visual mannerisms are the other 55%.

All too often, that critical first impression can turn to our disadvantage. Maybe a prospect doesn't like the way we walk or the colors we're wearing. Within the first few minutes of a personal visit, you may make a bad impression that can take years to correct.

But over the phone, all the prospect can do is hear you, not see you. With a pleasant voice and pleasing personality, you can lay the groundwork for a relationship free of personal prejudices.

You'll be judged not by how you look, but by what you know.

Is Versatile

In real estate, many of your calls will be to try to set up appointments. But don't overlook the wonderful versatility of the phone.

You can use the phone to do informal research, keep in touch with clients, qualify prospects quickly, and troubleshoot each transaction.

Moreover, putting your name and phone number on sign riders outside the homes you list or in advertisements can lead more prospective buyers and sellers straight to your desk.

Reaches More People

In face-to-face selling, salespeople average one interview for every five contacts they make. Over the phone, that ratio drops to one interview for every 10 prospects.

But the difference is that in pounding the pavement, a sales rep may drop in on five to eight potential customers a day. In an hour you can easily dial 20 to 25 numbers, probably talking to 15 or so prospects. From those 15 contacts, even an inexperienced salesperson will get perhaps one or two appointments; a pro should be able to set up one appointment from every five contacts.

If you have a farm with 300 homes, it would take you a month to drop by each house, assuming you could visit ten homes a day, seven days a week.

Over the phone, you could make the same number of contacts in half the time — maybe less.

You also wouldn't have to waste minutes aimlessly walking the streets and knocking on unanswered doors. In fact, it takes only 10 seconds to make a phone call.

Also, by calling first, you can effectively qualify your prospects — in other words, weed out those prospects who you know are going to wind up as dead ends.

Provides Immediate Feedback

One of the best things about the phone is that you know where you stand right away. By the time you hang up, you should know a little more about the person you talked to — hopefully, a lot more. They'll no longer be just a name or an address. You'll have formed an impression of who they are and what they're like, just by listening to their voice.

You should also have an idea of how you might be able to help them, whether now or a few years down the road.

Furthermore, by keeping careful records of your own performance, you'll be able to evaluate your skills over the phone and continuously sharpen them. If you've completed 10 calls and you're getting nowhere, with telemarketing you have the chance to rework your message.

Unlike direct mail, where you hit hundreds of homes at a time, using the phone allows you to catch and correct errors quickly.

That could mean rewriting your script or changing the time of day you're calling.

By the end of several sessions, you should have a good idea of what's motivating people to respond, and you can play it to the hilt.

Promotes Organized Professionalism

If you're well organized, you can take notes, refer to the Multiple Listing Book, look at computer printouts, update your appointment book, and check schedules — all without missing a beat while talking on the phone.

What's more, if you have more than one phone line in your office, you can even get immediate answers to a prospect's questions about which you need to call someone else, such as a mortgage broker or escrow officer.

All this helps you come across as more know-ledgeable and confident — and the person on the other end never needs to know how much help you have spread out in front of you.

Saves You Money

For most of us in the real estate business, the majority of our calls are local, which means the charges will be small. Moreover, these charges are probably being paid by your broker.

Within the first minute or so of the conversation, you should be able to tell if the person you're calling is a likely prospect. In addition, when we make a call that goes unanswered, there's no tab to be picked up by anyone.

Even when you consider the discount mailing rates for bulk materials, as an individual agent it's still often cheaper to let your fingers do the selling.

Is Personal

One important difference between telemarketing and direct mail is that the moment the person you're calling picks up the phone, you begin to build a relationship. You have the opportunity to talk about things like the weather, sports, or maybe something unusual that's happening in their neighborhood.

With all the calls you get from various kinds of salespeople around the country, imagine the impact it would have if a real estate agent called and began talking about what a great addition you put on your home; or the terrific paint job you had done last summer; or your pride and joy, the roses in the front yard.

If the agent came across sounding sincere and friendly, you would probably remember him or her and be willing to meet him or her (if, of course, you weren't already in the real estate business).

Real estate farming by phone lets you initiate and nourish these personal relationships that often lead to long-term clients.

One of the only ways your farm prospects are going to know how much you're doing for them — the only way they're going to keep feeling secure and trusting — is if you touch base with them often, and in a personal manner.

Keeping in Touch — An AT&T study claims that 68% of all customers drop away from businesses because they feel ignored or neglected.

With the phone, every call you make is a chance to let a potential buyer or seller know that you care about them and that you'll go the extra mile to help them.

With almost everyone in this country buying or selling a home every five years, we need to remember that if we do a good job selling ourselves and our services the first time around, the customer will be back again.

That's critically important when you consider a recent report in the *Los Angeles Times* which stated that 53% of the people move to a home within 10 miles of their previous home.

Sphere of Influence — Also important is the phone's ability to help broaden your *sphere of influence*. Every prospect has friends and family, and as you secure a relationship with your prospect, the chances for referrals also increase.

So you're not just building a relationship with one person, you're putting out your name and reputation before his family, friends, co-workers, and maybe even his barber.

And, if you haven't guessed by now, the perfect tool for this is the phone.

Targets Your Audience

As in direct mail, telemarketing allows you to pinpoint your efforts to a target audience.

Suppose, for example, you have prospective buyers who want a home in the Fair Oaks neighborhood because they like the schools. Maybe their hearts are set on a brick, two-story colonial with an attached garage.

Positive Impression	√
Breaks the Ice	√
Versatility	√
Reaches More People	√
Immediacy	√
Organized Professionalism	√
Low Cost	√
Personal Relationship	√
Targets Your Audience	√

For many reasons, telemarketing is the choice of today's busy sales professionals.

By driving around your farm (or neighborhood in general) you can write down the addresses of all those homes that fit the bill.

Checking in a "reverse" phone directory — one which lists phone numbers by address rather than by occupant's name — you can call the homeowners you've selected.

Even if they're not ready to list, it's a great way to get your name into someone's home.

Disadvantages of Telemarketing

The tremendous number of advantages should not cloud the disadvantages of telephone sales.

High Rejection Rate

It takes a certain amount of confidence to sit down at the phone, knowing that 9 out of every 10 people you call will tell you no. Being able to handle rejection professionally is what separates the top commission earners from run-of-the-mill agents.

Good agents know the rejection isn't personal; they just move on to the next call, with enthusiasm and optimism as strong as ever.

Less Personal Than Face-to-Face Visits

Farming phone calls are one step removed from the personal contact of a face-to-face visit — but you can make that distance work for you. Use it as a means of laying the groundwork for relationships without letting stereotypes or prejudices get in the way.

Doing this can make you much more effective when you finally visit the prospect's home.

Follow-Up Is Essential

The only way to make farming by phone work is to set a schedule and stick to it. And this isn't easy.

When you run into a string of busy signals or "no answers," you need to track them and make sure you reach the prospects. Often that's difficult, but it's necessary for farming success.

Telemarketing's Shady Past

All has not been rosy in the history of selling by telephone. In the '60s and early '70s, so-called boiler-room operations" hawking everything from swamp land in Florida to "free" trips to Las Vegas, gave telephone sales a bad name.

Fraud, particularly credit card fraud, ran rampant in the industry, and enforcement protection lagged behind — leaving many consumers holding the bag.

Fortunately, today things are much better. But still, it's not perfect by any means. Early in 1987 *Newsweek* magazine reported on a major scam produced by bogus "tour operators" who had managed to use phony travel discounts to bilk consumers out of tens of thousands of dollars nationwide.

Bringing this up is not meant to discourage you, but rather to make you aware of potential problems and possible perceptions in the marketplace.

You, as a local person who can interact with your farm by mail, in person, and by phone, have a tremendous advantage in overcoming the phone-only hurdle.

Types of Real Estate Telemarketing

In real estate, telemarketing can be divided into two types of calls: (1) outgoing and (2) incoming.

Outgoing Calls

During much of this book, we'll be discussing outgoing calls, the ones so often referred to as *cold calls*. Usually this kind of call is the agent's biggest fear and, as you'll see later, more likely than not, the fear is groundless.

Outgoing calls are used to keep in touch with sellers, make listing appointments, follow up referrals, bolster direct-mail results, strengthen ad campaigns, and do whatever else your creativity can dream up.

Incoming Calls

Incoming calls include: the person calling about a house described in a newspaper ad, someone responding to a letter you sent to your farm, inquiries about a "for sale" sign in the neighborhood, renters looking for homes, a friend referred by a happy client and, of course, complaints.

All too often, we tend to take incoming calls for granted, overlooking the fact that these are among the hottest leads we'll ever get. We make the mistake of thinking we've closed the deal just because they called, when in fact it's just a lead waiting to be closed.

So while this book will focus much of its attention on calls initiated by you, never overlook the importance of properly handling inbound calls as well.

Types of Calls in Real Estate Sales:

Outgoing	*Incoming*
Farm prospecting	*Response to ad*
Follow up referral	*Inquiry after drive-by*
For-Sale-By-Owner	*Referred by friend*
Keep in touch with customer	*Complaints*
Keep in touch with past clients	

Making the Telephone Work for You

Two important keys to making the telephone work for you include: having the right attitude toward the telephone and devoting the right amount of time to prospecting.

Check Your Attitude

Before you start serious farming by phone, you need to look at your own attitude toward the telephone. Is it easy for you to make calls? Do you feel like you're intruding into other people's lives?

If you do, that's sure to come across to anyone you call. And it will probably kill the root of this vital farming method.

Can you overcome it? Of course. But it may take considerable effort on your part.

To succeed over the phone, you must view it as a direct line to someone's heart and home. In a way, it's like a handshake — a personal expression of goodwill and greeting.

The telephone also has to take its rightful place among the tools of your trade; because if you don't people, and if you don't initiate the contact, chances are you won't make any sales.

Spend 75% of Your Time Prospecting

If you look around your office, you'll probably see most of the agents spending three quarters of their productive time doing paperwork, and only a quarter of their time looking for new clients and actually selling.

Wasted time is a key reason why the average full-time real estate salesperson in this country only makes about $18,000 a year.

If you want to succeed, you must turn this around and set aside 75% of your time for prospecting — much of it farming by phone — and cut the paperwork to just 25% of your time.

In the long run, this is the only way you're going to build up a solid base of income.

Summary

In this chapter you looked at how the growth of telemarketing is changing the way we do business in this country.

Versatile, inexpensive, and easy to use, selling by phone can generate leads, keep customers happy, qualify prospects, help research a market, target an audience, personalize a sales approach, and help arrange appointments.

For the real estate professional, using the phone saves time and money. It allows you to immediately assess the effectiveness of your sales message, and it helps you build a trusting relationship with your farm prospects.

Now that we've covered the basics of tele-marketing, it's time to move on to the specifics of how you can farm by phone.

4. Successful Phone Strategies

Before the first dial tone rings in your ear, take a moment to think about what you intend to accomplish over the phone.

Some of us think that talking comes as naturally as breathing — if you're one of these people, you're probably going to lose a lot of sales.

To succeed, you need a strategy — one that gives you realistic, achievable goals and, at the same time, puts you in the right frame of mind before that first call.

In the end, what you think and how you react can make a bigger difference than what you actually say.

How Much Is a Call Worth?

If you've tried farming by phone and haven't gotten very far, you may think of the calls as a waste of time.

Don't be so hasty. There's another way to look at the calls you make, one that will help you put them in the proper perspective. Here's an example:

Let's say that you're making cold calls two days a

week, two hours a day. For simplicity's sake, assume you call 15 people an hour and for every 15 calls, you set up one appointment. That adds up to two appointments a day, four appointments a week, 16 appointments a month.

Out of these 16 appointments, you close one sale, giving you a commission of $1,500 (assuming an average sales price of $100,000, with an average gross commission of 3%, and a 50/50 agent-broker split).

Looking back, you can see that for the 240 calls you made in the month (30 per day times 8 calling days per month), you make one sale. That means each call is worth about $6.25 ($1,500 commission divided by 240 calls) to you.

The figures we used are probably lower than what would actually happen. But the point is to think that you're getting paid not by the sale, but by the contact. And every contact means $6.25 in your pocket.

Usually, you should be able to count roughly on one sale for every 10 appointments you set, which would make each contact worth even more.

Your Greatest Telephone Challenge — You!

In telemarketing, your greatest challenge is not the person on the other end of the line. It's you.

Be Open to Rejection

It's tough to call people out of the blue. In a way, because the phone is one-to-one communication, you're sending a bit of yourself over the wire. To sell effectively, you can't be a mechanical voice or an impersonal order-taker. In this business, you have to express yourself. And that makes you personally vulnerable to rejection.

For anyone in telephone sales, rejection is a fact of life. If you're talking to 25 or 30 people an hour, chances are that 70% to 80% of them will say no.

But that's okay. You don't need for everyone to say yes. Unlike face-to-face sales, you're making contact with so many people each hour; so all you need is for one or two of them to say yes.

While that thought is comforting, don't set yourself up for rejection. Expect the best and, as Norman Vincent Peale writes, "In doing so, you bring everything into the realm of possibility."

Let Your Emotion Work for You

If you're afraid every time you sit down to begin calling, that fear will show up in your voice. Your caller will feel uncomfortable and find it easier to turn you down.

If you are nervous, let your nerves work for you. Deal with them the way an actor deals with stage fright — by allowing them to give you a competitive edge.

Channel that nervous energy into enthusiasm and watch the calls turn around. The way to conquer fear *isn't* by avoiding it, but by facing it and over-coming it.

If a prospect turns you down, don't take it per-sonally. They're not rejecting you, only the service you offer. It may be that in another week, month, or year, your phone will ring and they'll be on the other end, asking about buying or selling a home.

There are several ways to handle rejection, as discussed in many sales books and courses, but the single most important concept is to use rejection as a learning experience, and always keep a sense of humor as well as a separation from you the salesperson and what you are selling.

But each of us needs to use whatever works best for each of us personally.

The truth is, people are probably more approachable on the phone than you would imagine. And you'll find that hardly anyone ever says a direct no and hangs up.

Sounds odd, doesn't it? Although it's second nature for most people to reject any new idea that comes their way, they usually do it by raising an objection. And for every objection raised, there's a way for the creative seller to overcome it.

And always keep in mind that people generally do want to help you out.

Four "No's" Before One "Yes"

It also may give you a little comfort to know that even the top salespeople in this country don't usually close a deal until their fifth attempt. That means that for every "yes" they hear, they've already put four "no's" behind them.

Knowing the right way to handle rejection and overcoming the fear of failure are essential elements of success. But there are things you can do that will make it easier for you right from the start. And in the long run, you'll find yourself looking at rejection not as a negative experience, but as a positive one. Each rejection will become a personal challenge — and that's something you'll know how to handle.

Remember, for you, every day is a new beginning. When you leave the office, wipe the slate clean. Don't take lingering self-doubts, a shaky self-esteem, or feelings of failure home with you. Tomorrow is just around the corner.

By skillfully preparing a commercial property deal, in one day a 21-year-old real estate agent closed a sale that netted him $48,000.

Tomorrow you may get a call from a seller who wants to give you an exclusive listing on a half-million-dollar home.

Don't Limit Yourself

Unlike people who work for salaries, there's no limit to how much you can make; the only limitations are the ones you place on yourself. With almost everyone you know owning or wanting to own a piece of real estate, the possibilities are endless.

But all too often, we put limitations on ourselves without even realizing what we're doing. Aiming too low and lacking self-confidence are intangibles that tie us down even more tightly than a lack of leads.

To move ahead, you have to be willing to look at yourself objectively. Take into account your weaknesses, and compensate for them with your strengths.

Managing Your Time

If you think that following a schedule would crimp your style, think again. Planned or not, we all live on schedules. If you don't sketch out your time in advance, you're probably wasting a lot more of it than you realize.

Time is something all of us have in equal measure. Making the best use of their time is where the pros stand out from the run-of-the-mill agents.

Set an Overall Objective

When you approach farming by phone, first you need to decide on an overall objective. Rather than going for the once-in-a-lifetime sale, most of us should set our sights on using farming calls primarily to arrange appointments.

When comparing making appointments to dropping by unannounced, remember that making an appointment subtly tells a prospect you appreciate the value of his or her time. And unconsciously, your prospect also places a premium on the value of your time. Frankly, given our hectic work schedules today, I think most of us regard the unexpected visitor as an annoyance, not a welcome guest.

How many times have you hidden inside, not answering the door, because it was so obviously a salesperson standing there? Or how many times have you spotted a piece of "junk mail" and tossed it into your trash without a glance? But I bet you could count on one hand the number of times you've let the phone ring and ring, as you stood by without answering.

There is something very compelling about the ring of the phone. On the other end could be news that you've won a sweepstakes, gotten a promotion, or have a new baby granddaughter. And you'll never know unless you pick up the receiver.

In the right hands, the phone becomes a powerful sales tool — one that's perhaps more effective than any other.

Plan Ahead

Now that you've decided to use the phone as part of your sales strategy, look at the year ahead of you.

Don't take your sales strategy day by day. Work it out for the months to come. But be flexible enough to change it when the need arises.

In the beginning, you may decide simply to call every home in your farm. A good rule of thumb is to touch base with your farm by calling every three months.

This time, maybe you're following up a letter or maybe not. But you've decided that you're going to do your best to speak to every person living in your area. And you're going to try to set up face-to-face meetings as soon as possible — hopefully to fill up your next week. Where do you start?

First, in your heart, make a commitment that you'll finish what you start. It is easy to get discouraged, but quitters never go anywhere. So look at the next few weeks and begin developing your strategy. You'll be surprised at how much you wind up accomplishing.

In most areas of the country, the months of June and July are good times to prospect for listings. That's when families have some time off, the kids are out of school, and people are more willing to contemplate a move. Another good month is February, after the hectic pace of the holiday season has slowed down.

So you will want to schedule some farming by phone the last week of January and at the beginning of June.

Then thinking back over all the ways companies are using telemarketing, you know that you can boost the response from your direct mailings if you follow them up with a phone call.

Follow-up calls should be scheduled about three to four days after a letter arrives, so the homeowner has time to open it and read it, but not forget it.

Of course there are other opportunities to plan for. Your firm or franchise affiliation may be planning a big ad campaign, tied into the local media, running a series of feature stories on new developments in the area or the real estate market in general. The week after that would also be a good time to get on the phone.

If you've been in real estate longer than a year, you know which months are your best and which are slow. Use your slow times to generate leads for the more productive times.

Plan in advance and you won't find yourself scrambling for prospects.

Draw Up a Daily Plan

Practically speaking, you'll probably want to restrict your calling to two hours a day. Even telemarketing pros start to fade fast after four hours. And whenever your voice begins to lose its enthusiasm, letting boredom show through, it's best to stop.

In deciding when to call, certain times are better than others: "fringe" times — mid-morning, late afternoon, or weekends (except Sunday before noon) — are generally good.

Going back to our original figures from Chapter 3, you know that you can plan on calling about 20 numbers each hour.

If you don't have a touch-tone phone, get one. You can dial three times as fast as with a rotary phone. Dialing one number takes 10 seconds, and every second you can save adds up to minutes you can spend selling.

Calling 20 numbers an hour, two hours a day, multiplies out to 40 calls a day or 200 calls a week. If your farm has 300 homes, it will take you a little more than a week to reach all of them — two weeks, if you add in a few days for callbacks.

Farm Call Plan

Farm Call Plan

Date: _____

Farm Area _____

1. Number of Homes in Farm _____

2. Hours Calling Per Day _____

3. Number of Calls Per Hour _____

4. Calls Per Day (2 x 3) _____

5. Number of Days to Reach Total Farm (1 ÷ 4)

_____

6. Plus 2 Days for Call-backs Equal Total ____

Follow-up _____

_____

_____

_____

Other Notes _____

_____

_____

_____

_____

_____

The Farm Call Plan worksheet helps you determine the number of calls you need to make to reach you entire farm each month.

Set a Performance Goal

Each day when you make calls, it's important that you have a goal. Most of us would probably set as our objective a certain number of calls. Don't.

If you do that, you'll deprive yourself of the satisfaction of a job well done; because your sense of accomplishment won't come with the completion of a call, but with the scheduling of an interview.

Your goal needs to be a *performance goal.* In your mind, every time you sit down to begin phoning, say to yourself, "I'm going to schedule two appointments today." Or "I'm going to get five referrals."

Then don't stop until you've reached your goal.

Make Short Calls

Since most people have an attention span of only four minutes over the phone, you'll want to keep your calls short. But that doesn't mean they shouldn't be warm and personal. Keeping your time limits in mind will help you make your calls more efficiently and they'll produce better results.

Call Everybody and Keep Moving

As you work your way through the list you're calling, you'll probably find yourself wanting to skip certain names or addresses. That's another no-no. Being committed means sticking to what you've said you're going to do.

If you start cheating yourself on the small things, it'll be easier to cheat yourself on the bigger things ahead. The only person you're hurting by doing a sloppy job is yourself.

Another trick is to keep right on moving. If you're feeling great because you just lined up an unexpected interview, don't treat yourself to a cup of coffee or brag about it to your co-workers.

Your best chance for setting up another call is right after you hang up from your first success. As the old saying goes, "Strike while the iron is hot."

On the other hand, if you find yourself running into a series of rejections, don't stop to feel sorry for yourself. Dial the next number right away. If you give in to self-pity, it will start feeding on itself and mushroom into a cloud of negative feelings that will kill any potential prospects you reach.

Track Your Progress

As you're working your way through your list of calls, it's a good idea to keep track of how you're doing. The sample form on the next page is an easy way for you to track your results at a glance.

Your tracking need not be elaborate or formal. Just use old-fashioned scratches (/////) on the appropriate lines.

If you spot a pattern showing that something's not working out, stop and make changes. If you notice that at a certain time of day, you're running into a lot of busy signals, switch your calling time.

While you're talking to someone, you should be jotting down notes on the card you keep for each family in your farm.

When you've finished talking, if you've run into an objection, jot it down in one word in the appropriate section of the form. That way at the end of the session, you'll be able to see immediately what your major roadblocks are.

Call Response Tally

Call Resonse Tally

Date: _____

Farm Area _____

Time of Day _____

Number of Calls _____

Calls Completed _____

Busy Signals _____

Left Message _____

Call Backs _____

Referrals _____

Objections _____

Appointments _____

Follow-up _____

_____

_____

_____

Other Notes _____

_____

_____

_____

The Call Response Tally sheet shown above allows you to keep track of your calls as you're making them.

You can also spot at a glance your accomplishments over the past two hours. Callbacks, referrals, appointments — all of them are signs that you're heading in the right direction. And if you keep careful records, you're sure to see that your results gradually improve over the months and years to come.

Follow Through

When you call it quits for the day, your phone farming isn't over. Block out a half hour for followup. Maybe you've promised to send someone some listings on new homes. Or one of the callers requested more information on a financing program your firm offers. Or perhaps you found a prospective seller who'd like to have one of your company brochures.

If you want to make a terrific impression, do something hardly anyone else does anymore: Follow through right away. The sooner you get the material in the mail, the sooner you have another reason to call again.

That brings up an important point. In real estate, it's especially important that you return calls right away. Making a prospective client wait a few hours or a few days to hear from you — some agents don't get around to returning calls for a few weeks! — can destroy whatever trust you're trying to build. It's like saying to someone, "You're not important enough for me to call back right away." That's something none of us like to feel.

If you find your schedule so packed that returning calls immediately is impossible, then be sure to set aside some time each day just for calls. Usually 45 minutes to an hour is enough. Call people back even if you have to do it during the evening. In the long run, the few minutes you spend returning a call can lead to thousands of dollars in commissions down the road.

If you've dropped some material in the mail or promised someone you'd get back in touch with them in a few days, make a note of it. Write it on your schedule on the day you think is best, and stick to that schedule.

Other Time Management Tips

You should probably schedule a drive through your farm area at least once a week. Then you can look for new "for sale" signs, "for sale by owner" signs, a remodeling project, or perhaps something about an individual home that stands out. Any scrap of knowledge can be useful, as you'll see when we get into what to say on your calls.

To keep all this straight, everyone in the real estate business needs an ample calendar book, with enough space to write down all the pertinent information every day. It's also handy if you can keep a phone listing under the same cover. And make sure you write *your* name, address, and phone number on the first page. Notebooks are easy to forget, and with your name on it, there's at least a chance someone will pick it up and try to return it to you.

At the end of each day, in your mind, go back over the results of your calls. Go back over your Call Response Tally. See if anything stands out and look for ways that you could do things better tomorrow.

If you've done all you could, if you feel that you gave it your best shot, then be content.

Success is a series of small steps that, in the long run, make a big difference.

Be Prepared

Before you begin your farming by phone, make sure you're ready. That means doing your homework.

It's easy to throw a list of phone numbers together and think that's all you need. Doing so is a sure prescription for failure.

In the first place, you're positioning yourself as an expert in the minds of people you call. You're a specialist in a complicated field that many of them probably don't understand a lot about (although they'd never admit it). You're not a person peddling houses or listings; you're a competent, knowledge-able agent whose primary interest is helping your clients make sound real estate decisions. For that attitude to come across, you can't fake it. You have to know your facts, and those facts must be current.

Off the top of your head, you should be able to describe what kinds of financing options are available, any new developments under way, home values this month, average rental values, current changes in legislation, daily fluctuations in mortgage rates, and the latest listings to come into your office.

Once you've mastered all this, you'll be amazed at how much you know and have to talk about. Plus, you'll have the added advantage of a great boost to your self-esteem.

When you feel you've finished your research — a process, by the way, that you should never stop — enough to begin calling, the next step is to prepare your directory.

Also nearby should be pens, pencils, a calendar, and your appointment book. During calls, I find it works best to jot down most of my notes in pencil, using the pen to highlight areas that need my attention later.

Here's a handy checklist of items you should have

ready before you dial that first number:

1. Farm phone directory
2. Calendar
3. Appointment book
4. Pens and pencils (sharp)
5. Notepad
6. Call Response Tally sheets
7. Multiple Listing Book

In addition, make sure there's no radio or TV in the background. Music may be soothing for you, but to your prospect, it smacks of unprofessionalism.

Of course, you also need to know what you're going to say. That's what the bulk of this book will help you with.

The Successful Sales Presentation

In essence, there are certain qualities in a sales presentation that make it work.

Reflects Prior Planning — You have to know your business so well that there's nothing a prospect can ask you that you can't answer. Your initial approach needs to be smooth, confident, and so well practiced that it's second nature to you.

Projects You as an Expert — We've already talked about the facts; this refers more to an attitude. If you love your business and you're good at it, you can't help but transfer those feelings to whomever you're talking to.

Reveals a Philosophy of Selling — This point is crucial, because this separates you from all the other people who try to sell their services. Your job is to help people find out what they really want, then make sure they get it. That's a lot different from approaching a prospect as your next commission check.

Creates a Sense of Urgency — When it comes to selling or listing homes, it's hard to push a time limit. But some of you have the advantage of a rapidly moving market, and all of us have the fact that each home is unique and others are interested.

Sounds Spontaneous and Sincere — It's ironic that in selling, the more you practice, the more spontaneous you can sound. Although it may seem that spontaneity and sincerity are traits you can't manufacture, the fact is that you can. I'll never forget an essay in *Time* magazine some years back that listed a whole series of thoughts to ponder. The one I remember is "Sincerity is not the measure of truth."

Twist that around and you'll realize that sincerity is something we can practice and practice effectively.

Is Always Honest — A good agent never fails to point out material drawbacks that may affect a sale. Even with the disclosure statements sellers fill out, things get overlooked. If a buyer asks, it's up to you to know. And if you're misinformed or you deliberately mislead a prospect, they'll never darken your door again — and you might be in for trouble along the legal front, too.

I remember back a number of years ago when I bought my college sweetheart a diamond ring. Not knowing anything about the "four C's" (cut, clarity, color, and caret weight), I was looking only at size.

The jeweler was writing up the order for a ring when I spotted one almost exactly the same but three times as expensive. So I asked the salesman why. And he replied quite matter-of-factly, "Well, that one doesn't have any inclusions (flaws) in it."

Perhaps needless to say, I had him cancel the order, and I then found a jeweler who gave me the full story up front.

Avoids Stereotypes — Before you take the plunge and pick up the phone, remember to clear your mind. Remove all the stereotypes and preconceptions you have about people.

The used car salesman you call may have a hobby of collecting rare, antique stamps. Or the college professor may spend his weekends coaching a Little League team. Or the housewife may, in reality, be the financial whiz who prudently invests and monitors her doctor-husband's six-figure income.

In sales, you can't afford to offend or write off anyone. That reminds me of the rock star who walked into a fashionable boutique in London.

With his long, unkempt hair, his jeans, and wrinkled shirt, he looked like he spent his nights sleeping in a cardboard box on the sidewalk.

As he wrote out a check for several thousand dollars, the salespeople in the shop were a little nervous. But they had the sense to know that appearances can be deceiving. As a result, they held back and didn't spoil a large sale. Chances are that rock star will shop in that boutique again.

Each of us is a unique individual, worthy of the best service we can give. If anyone should realize that, it's the person who's in the business of selling homes. People see their homes as an extension of themselves.

Even a tract home becomes an expression of the owner's personality. Never prejudge a prospect because of what they do or who you think they are.

A long time ago, the Golden Rule was laid down as a guiding principle for human relationships. It's as true today as it was then. "Treat others the way that you would want them to treat you."

Cultivating that attitude is critical, because your clients are the most important people in your business world. After all, they're the ones who send you your paychecks.

If you make up your mind to like people, they'll like you back. And when people like you and trust you, they'll give you their home to sell.

The Power of Positive Thinking

When you start thinking about the time it will take to send letters to 300 or more homes, personally call each one, work the floor, and follow up leads, it can easily seem overwhelming.

But if you take it one step at a time, it can be done. The key is that you have to *believe* you'll be able to do it.

You know, it's not the hard work that wears us out. It's the emotional ups and downs that make us tired quicker than anything else.

All of us need to believe in ourselves. We can't depend on a husband or wife, a co-worker, or a friend to give us the strength we need to face each day. They won't always be around at that critical moment when we hang up the phone or walk away from a closed door.

To succeed in sales, you have to have the spunk to know you'll make it — that sense of assuredness no one else can give you. You can only find it for yourself.

If you think you're going to fail, you will. If you're sure success is just around the corner, chances are it will be.

Top salespeople feel in their bones that anyone who turns them down is making a mistake, because after all, the salesperson is only trying to do what's best for them.

Every great salesperson is characterized by a genuine interest in and concern for the people they do business with. They remember people's names and faces; they write down their hobbies and important information about their families. Often they remember their birthdays.

All of us want more than just a paycheck at the end of a deal. We want a sense of satisfaction, the feeling of a job well done.

Achieving that takes work. And from now on, we'll be getting into the nuts and bolts of how to help both your income and self-esteem grow.

Summary

In this chapter, we covered a lot of ground, much of it dealing with the right mind-set for approaching your telephone farming.

To begin with, think of each contact you make as something you're getting paid for, because if you don't make those contacts, you won't have any sales. Focusing on the contacts puts the emphasis where it belongs. As an old-time salesman once said, "Meet with twenty people belly-to-belly every day and success is guaranteed."

Times have changed and the days of door-to-door peddling are disappearing. But even with the increased reliance on the phone, contacts still come first.

To capsulize your basic preparation for farming by phone, here's a short list:

1. Decide to make a definite number of calls each day.
2. Schedule a definite time period to make your calls.
3. Set a performance goal for yourself, with a certain number of appointments or referrals you want to have by the end of the session.
4. Finish all of the calls on your list each session.
5. Keep track of how you're doing with a Call Response Tally sheet.
6. Strike while the iron is hot. When you get an appointment, dial another number quickly.
7. When you run into a dead end, dial another number quickly.
8. Don't stop to analyze your results during your session; wait until the end of the day.

Finally, and most important, every time you pick up the phone, believe you're going to take the first step toward a sale. Be enthusiastic about what you're doing, show that enthusiasm in your voice, and you'll find it's contagious.

Showing great heart and spirit will make you stand out in the crowd of realtors clamoring for listings. And having the best heart, the most captivating spirit, means that you're always looking out for the other person's interests.

Cultivate a belief in yourself — with a genuine caring for others. Do all you can to become an expert in your field, and no one will be able to hold you back.

5. Your Farm Phone Directory

Of course, it's impossible to get started farming by phone without an updated list of names and numbers of everyone who lives in your farm. Putting this list together will take some time, but once it's finished, it becomes your most valuable resource of all — a gold mine just waiting to be tapped.

Getting Your Original Directory

When you're sitting at your desk, staring at the map of your farm area, wondering how on earth you can possibly find all those phone numbers, don't despair. It's easier than you think.

Territorial Farms

If you've selected a territorial farm, your first job is to contact your local title company. They keep records, according to each street address, giving the name of the owner, mailing address for tax purposes, purchase price, last date of sale, first date of sale, and a brief legal description of the property.

You could compile your own list, if you want to spend hours pouring over records in the County Assessor's Office. But why should you, when the title company has the information so near at hand? However, the County Assessor's records may come into play if you want more specific information about a particular property such as permits given for room additions or remodeling.

If your office belongs to the Multiple Listing Service (MLS), the same tax information available through the title company may be on your computer.

Now that you've got the addresses, what about the phone numbers?

No, you don't have to spend the next week shuffling through your local phone directory, getting frustrated. Neither do you have to spend time and money calling information — at 50¢ a call in this area, finding 300 numbers could cost a fortune!

Your next step is calling the directory services department of your local phone company. They publish *reverse* or *street address directories* for every area they serve.

In the Los Angeles area, Pacific Bell keeps street address directories for the entire country.

Each directory covers the same territory as your local phone book; only instead of looking up someone's last name, you check their address. In a matter of minutes, you can have the phone numbers of everyone on a block.

Pacific Bell updates the directory every six months for most cities, every three months for major metropolitan areas. There's no one time of the year when directories are issued.

But unlike your local phone book, these aren't free. Pacific Bell customers have to *lease* the directory, paying anywhere from $39 to $132 per edition.

One problem you could run into is a rash of unlisted numbers. If you do, there's no way you can get the numbers out of the phone company.

But be creative. If you have a substantial percentage of unlisted numbers, why not consider a special mailing to these prospective clients, offering a small premium if they return a prepaid card with basic information: size of family, size of house, occupation, and phone number?

Going this route, one thing you can be sure of is that they haven't had many other agents calling them. So the extra effort may pay off.

If you select as your territorial farm a certain subdivision or condominium complex, chances are you'll be able to pick up a homeowner's directory with names, addresses, and phone numbers. It may even have the size of the family. Finding one of these directories can make this stage of your work a lot easier.

There are other sources of lists of names and addresses, but not in a form so convenient for you to use in farming. And only a few include phone numbers.

Social Farms

If you've chosen the route of social farming your approach to getting names, addresses, and phone numbers is, by necessity, a little different.

Most organizations and clubs publish a membership list, similar to the homeowner's directory, with names, addresses, phone numbers, family members, and whatever information they think important.

If the club or organization you choose as your social farm doesn't have a membership list, you can always volunteer to make one up. Just be sure you have the time. Looking up several hundred names in the phone book can take days, not to mention the strain on your eyes. So try to avoid this if you can.

Before moving into what to do with your list once you get it, here's a final reminder. Lists of names and addresses are the bread and butter of many American businesses.

All too often, we unthinkingly throw them out. Maybe you have a list from a former employer, a scout troop one of your children belongs to, a volunteer association you or your spouse may participate in.

Today we have local clubs for everything from BMW owners to people who grow orchids for a hobby. If you aren't a member, maybe one of your friends or neighbors is. Maybe they'll let you copy one of their directories. In this business, you can't afford to overlook any opportunity to put out your name.

Maintaining Your Directory

You can maintain your farm directory in one of two ways: (1) on computer or (2) manually, typically using a index card file.

Computerized Directories

Using a personal computer makes sense, if you're familiar with them. There are several software programs especially designed for real estate farming, and many off-the-shelf data base programs can also suit your needs.

With these programs, you can readily sort your farm by name, address, city, contact date, zip code, or miscellaneous characteristics, such as home type, square footage, or loan data.

However, computers cost money and, more than anything else, it takes time to learn how to operate them. One agent I know started in real estate and went out and bought a personal computer. Instead of prospecting for sales and listings, he spent his first two months learning how to run his computer — which proved to be costly.

Manual Directories

For most of us, keeping records manually is simplest. For one thing, your farm has to be a manageable size. It's not like you're trying to keep track of several thousand names.

So that brings us to the bulwark of any good filing system: the index card.

Some realtors use 3-by-5 cards, others prefer 4-by-6 cards so they can take more notes. Frankly, I'd opt for the latter. The more you know and write down about the people who live in your farm, the more you'll have to talk to them about. And the more substantive things you have to talk about, the better the chances are that you'll develop a relationship and eventually get their listing.

For your farm itself, start off with index cards arranged in alphabetical order, by name. That makes it easy for you to find a card quickly when a prospect calls in.

To save time and trouble, I recommend using peel-off mailing labels for your master file cards.

All you have to do is type a master of your mailing list on blank paper, in the proper format to align with the labels, then have it copied onto the peel-off label sheets at your local quick printer.

While you're having labels made for a first mailing, have two extra sets made — one for your index cards and a second one to keep in a safe place at home.

You probably also should have the printer copy the basic form (see below for sample) for your index card, so you don't have to type hundreds of them by yourself.

On the back of the card, I would jot down all further contacts — specifying the date and nature of them. For example: 3/12/87 letter, 7/15/87 call, etc.

Manual Farm From

Manual Farm Form		Joe Prospect 123 Way Street Anytown, USA 12345
Phone Number _____		
Husband's Job _____	Wife's Job _____	
Interests _____		
Kids _____		
Type of House _____		
First Contact Date _____ (see next contact on back)		
Date _____ Comments _____		

The Manual Farm From shown above is designed to help keep track of your contact with your farm prospects, either by phone, by mail, or in person. The front side has the basic information; while on the back, you keep track of more detailed data in chronological order.

Next to the date and nature of contact, I would mark down notes, such as any birthdays, trips, hobbies, or special interests they mention. The more you know about them, the better off you'll be. It's remarkable what a timely birthday card can do to build up your relationship.

When you talk to someone on the phone, if they raise objections to your sales presentation (as most people usually do), briefly write them down, as well as the outcome of the call. Knowing what objections people raise, as we'll see later, can be a key to finding their "hot buttons" in buying or selling their home.

Even if you don't succeed in setting up an appointment with them on the first call, you'll be much more prepared the next time around.

As a postscript, remember how important it is to keep track of whom you call and when. There's nothing quite as embarrassing as calling the same person twice in one week with the same opening line. That's a sure way to kill a prospect forever.

As to where and how to keep your farm directory, that's up to you. Just be sure it's safe.

Buyer Files

In addition to your directory, you should consider keeping two other sets of files.

The first is for when a prospect turns into a buyer. At that point, the information on your Manual Farm Form isn't enough. Later we'll discuss how to use the form we suggest below for handling incoming calls, but for now, let's just think about it as a way to keep track of what the buyers we represent are looking for.

Buyer File Form

Date _____ Ad Reference _____

Property Called About _____

Name _____

Address _____

City/State/Zip _____

Phone (Home) _____ (Work) _____

Jobs (Husband) _____ (Wife) _____

Family Size _____ Current Home: Owns ____ Rents ____

Desired Area _____ House Type _____

Price Range _____ VA? _____ FHA? _____

Special Features Wanted _____

_____

Comments _____

_____

Buyer File Form lets you keep track of when a prospect turns into a buyer.

Again, on the back of this card, I recommend keeping a list of all contacts, with special notes to help you remember more about the buyers and what they want in their next home.

As for the third type of file, earlier we mentioned jotting down in your schedule book times when you promised to call someone back.

Tickler Files

One thing that has worked well for me over the years is a special, chronological (or *tickler*) file for each month. You can buy the accordion (folding) files at your local stationery store or make one of your own using manila folders.

These files are marked 1 through 31, and for each date you need to do something for a prospect or client, simply slip a note to yourself into the appropriate file. It's handy because you can attach all the information you need, and that saves you the time of looking it up.

At the back of the file, I stick notes for the months, even years, ahead. Then at the end of the month, I go through these and file the ones that are for the month coming up next.

It's a very simple process, but you won't believe how efficient it makes you. All you have to do is get into the habit of taking notes.

Updating Your Directory

If the phone numbers in your farm file are from a reverse or street address directory, even with revisions every six months, there's a likelihood some of the numbers will be out of date.

If you're using numbers from a commercial list broker or a membership roster published once a year, chances are even better that you'll hit it wrong.

That's why it's important to keep records. On your first call, you'll want to check to see that the information you have is accurate. But you can also update your records *before* you call.

Before You Call

Before you even approach the phone, it might be a good idea to send out a direct-mail letter first, requesting address correction service through the post office. By doing this, at least you'll have the right name with each address (hopefully).

71

If you have to, you can call information for the new number.

If you call a home in your farm and there's a forwarding number, before dialing check your local directory to see what neighborhood the first three digits are in. Then you'll know whether they moved two blocks away or across town. That could make a difference in deciding whether to follow up.

During That Critical First Call

On that critical first call, you should verify the information you have and fill in the blanks for the rest of it.

For example, ask about the children, their names and ages; the number of people in the family; special features in their home; hobbies; how long they've lived in the neighborhood; why they chose that particular house; and the story of how they bought it. Ask whatever fits naturally into the flow of the conversation.

However, before you dial you should at least know the type of home they're living in and should've filled in that blank on your Manual Farm Form.

Whenever you call, it's important to be sensitive to the fact that there could have been sudden changes in the family.

Perhaps the marriage is breaking up and the husband or wife has moved out. Maybe they've temporarily rented out their home. Or perhaps it has been sold and is still in escrow. Or there could have been a death in the family.

You should always check your local paper for special events like marriages, births, deaths, and send appropriate cards. Today, not even all our close personal friends remember them. It's another way to show you care.

Finally, keeping your records up-to-date is a good incentive for you to set up a regular schedule for farming by phone. As I suggested earlier, once every three months seems about right. But depending on circumstances, you may want to call even more often.

Expanding Your Directory

By now, I hope you're convinced the telephone is one of the most important tools of your trade.

It can be used in a variety of ways, from beefing up your advertising results to offering congratulations on the wedding of a son or daughter of someone who lives in your farm.

Think about the telephone as your almost cost-free way to keep in touch, and then think about all the situations in which you can use it.

Offer Toll-Free Lines

According to AT&T, using a toll-free "800" number in your print and direct-mail ads can increase response 25% to 30%.

Depending on your market, you might want to consider this, especially if you live in an area where any call 15 miles away is a toll call.

One company, Hotline Exchange of St. George, Utah, offers real estate firms a special "800" service at very reasonable rates. A special operator takes down the caller's name, phone number, and the property he or she is interested in. After the operator hangs up, he or she immediately phones your office with the information. This service takes calls seven days a week.

Using this type of service can make your operation

seem larger and more trustworthy in the minds of prospective clients. It also can generate more leads for you — many of them from qualified buyers or sellers.

Broadcast Your Name and Number

As for putting your name and phone number into circulation, earlier we mentioned using sign riders on the "for sale" signs of homes you list. This is a must if it's allowed in your area.

Also, you should pass out your business card (with your phone number on it) every opportunity you get, even at your dry cleaners. You never know who's in the market for a home.

Keep in Contact

You'll want to call your past clients about every six months or so, partly as a gesture of friendship, but also as a practical business matter.

Perhaps they're beginning to think about moving, or a job transfer is coming up, or they know someone else who just began looking for a house. The possibilities are limitless, and the only way you're going to find out about them is by keeping in touch.

There are also some practical times, such as holidays or special events, when you should re-establish contact.

Track Expired Listings

Among the most common and least sought-after leads, of course, are expired listings. Those you can find easily with the help of the Multiple Listing Book and careful tracking.

Chances are that the problem wasn't with the house, but with an agent who didn't give the listing his or her full attention. Or, quite often it may just be a lack of communication between the owner and the agent.

Walk this ground delicately, but be aware that you could help reap the harvest.

Watch for FSBO's

As anyone who has ever put up a "for sale by owner" sign knows, the one thing it's sure to attract are local real estate agents anxious to get the listing.

We'll go into this in depth later, but keep FSBO homes on your list of possibilities.

And remember, if someone does want to sell their own home and save a 6% commission, there's always the possibility you can make an arrangement to help them with the paperwork for a reduced fee or help them find a new home.

Wherever there's a seller, there's usually a buyer. It just depends on how you look at it.

Suggest Refinancing

Another time to contact a past client is when there's a junior trust deed due. Perhaps they're interested in selling to avoid a big balloon payment.

Or if your notes show that a client is paying a mortgage at 14% and rates are dropping, maybe they'd rather move up to a more expensive home (keeping their monthly mortgage payment roughly the same) than refinance.

In addition, of course, dropping interest rates

generally make for a stronger sales market as well. It's worth a call to find out.

Visit Neighbors of a Listing

When you get a new listing in your farm, before putting up the sign, take a few hours to call or visit the neighbors across the street and on the same block.

Tell them that the house is going up for sale. That's a simple courtesy, and most people are curious at least about the asking price. At the same time, you can inquire as to whether they have any friends or relatives who might be interested in moving to that neighborhood or at least attending an open house.

It's another good way to get to know the people who live in your farm.

Watch for Special Events

Sometimes you may spot a story about a big celebrity moving to town. Celebrities need houses just like everybody else — and who's better qualified to show them around than you are?

Maybe your farm's school system just hired a new superintendent from out of state. What harm is there in checking with a school board member or reporter to get the superintendent's phone number and give him or her a call?

As the old saying goes, "It's the early bird who catches the worm." To do your best in today's real estate market, you have to explore every avenue you can think of. Don't do only what everybody else does, do your own thing and see how well it works.

Knowing Your Farm

One of the key advantages of operating a territorial farm is that you can know it inside out. At first, what follows may seem like a lot of work, but it isn't. Noticing what's happening in the neighborhood your farm covers will soon become second nature.

Why? Because when you care about people, you care about the things that are important to them. And from your standpoint, there are certain basic things that everyone who lives in your farm is concerned about. So you are, too.

Keep Up on Current Events

Let's begin with the simple suggestion of reading your local paper, especially the pages that focus on community news. That's a good way to get the names of influential people in the area (potential clients, perhaps?) and clues to the character of the community.

A bedroom suburb of Dallas will have concerns much different from inner-city Detroit. It's up to you to know what those concerns are.

Probably the most useful information you can have readily at hand is a ranking of the scholastic achievement rates in the schools within your farm area.

Time and time again, the first thing any parent wants to know when they're becoming interested in a house is, "How are the schools?"

In my community, those statistics are published every fall in the local paper. It's a simple matter to keep copies in your office.

If the schools are not that good, often there's an

77

excellent private school nearby. You should know what kind of program it offers, the approximate cost, and volunteer that information if appropriate.

You also need to be familiar with where most of the people who live in your farm work. Do they make a 40-mile daily commute into a major city? If so, are there commuter buses?

Do most of them work at a big factory or plant in the same neighborhood? If so, how's that industry doing?

If you were trying to sell homes in the steel town of Gary, Indiana, a few years back, you should've planned some alternate source of income for awhile.

If a factory in your farm is opening up a new division, maybe you could contact plant officials about helping the new employees find homes when they relocate.

As an agent who specializes in that particular area, you must stay up on the major hospitals, prominent doctors, and clinics. It would also be a good idea to read any feature stories in the local paper about the neighborhood Easter Seal Center or special programs. You never know when the parent of a disabled child will walk through your door.

You should also be familiar with the nitty-gritty details of everyday life, such as trash pickup, sewer or septic service, and any problems at the water company.

Now on none of these things do you have to be an expert, but you should know enough to give a knowledgeable response when asked. Remember, you're the expert on your farm area.

Know the Positive Aspects of Negative Features

A word of caution: If some of the homes in your farm have a terrible location problem — for example, being smack in the middle of a landing pattern to a major airport or within sniffing distance of the local landfill — don't try to hide it.

If planes are a problem, point out how few minutes they're overhead when they come in to land. If it's the landfill, play up the reduced price or talk about future plans to turn it into a golf course (if that's true).

If you don't mention it, you know they'll find out. And five years from now, when they're looking for a more spacious and more expensive home, you can be sure they'll have thrown your card away.

Almost any negative feature has a positive aspect, if you take the time to look for it. And if you bring such things up first, not only will it help your credibility with your prospects, but it will also help overcome objections which may be raised down the line.

Keep Abreast of Changes

In the last chapter, I mentioned the importance of driving through your farm once a week.

When you do, look for things like a new garage, a fresh paint job, recently bricked sidewalks, a renovated family room, a major addition, ground tilled for a garden, or nice new landscaping.

When you see something that stands out, have a clipboard and paper handy to take notes. Jot down the address and the feature that interested you. Back at the office, if you don't know the prospect right off, look the address up in your reverse directory.

When you've found the name, go to your farm directory, and make a note on that person's index card.

79

All of this will take perhaps a few minutes, but imagine the difference it will make when you call and speak to the owners about the possibility of helping them with their real estate needs.

By remarking on specific features of their house, you'll start off right, letting them know that to you, a client is someone who deserves individual, personal attention. And that will give you an edge hard for any other agent to match.

Once you've begun finding out more about your farm, you'll develop a genuine interest in the area and its people. After all, selling their homes is your bread and butter. What involves them involves you.

Let Your Farm Know You

You not only have to know your farm, the people in your farm also have to know you.

This is the area where many agents fail. It's tough to make cold calls or go knocking on doors. But that's the only way you'll ever be more than a name to your farm. How often the people who live there will mention your name and in what context is up to you.

Right now, I live in an area that has one real estate agent who almost exclusively gets every listing. She can walk down the street and tell you about every person who lives in each house — what they do for a living, if they play loud music, if they have children, what kind of flowers they grow, if they're renting or buying, *and* if they're thinking about moving.

She knows almost everyone. And everyone knows her. When it comes time to sell a home, why would they go to anyone else? The commissions are all the same. But this agent knows the area, its problems, and its people intimately. She's not just an agent, she's a friend.

As a real estate professional cultivating a farm, your job is to become a friend to as many people there as you can.

That doesn't mean you spend so much time being neighborly and helpful that it takes away from your work, but a few minutes of kindness each day can give you a wonderful feeling inside and lead to steady commissions.

If you practice being nice to people, you'll find that the world is full of interesting folks, whether it's waiters, bus drivers, or the clerk at the nearby convenience store. And it never hurts to give each and every one of them a business card with your name and number.

Don't narrow your world to people you separate neatly into their own little categories: potential clients, friends, relatives, and service people.

Treat each person with the attention and respect we all deserve, and you'll see your farm directory grow by leaps and bounds.

Summary

In this chapter, you learned the nuts and bolts of putting together your farm directory.

First, you saw what a great help your title company can be in finding records for you. Then you turned to the phone company for a street address directory to give you the phone numbers.

Once the basic data is in your hands, it's time to put together a file, usually on 4-by-6 index cards, that includes every home in your farm.

That file is the backbone of your business. Not only does it enable you to keep track of names and addresses, it also helps you remember personal things about the people in your farm.

From the beginning, it's important to verify that the information you have is correct, and also to expand that information with your first call.

You also need to make sure you call on a regular schedule, double-checking your facts each time. In all of our lives, things can change overnight.

Finally, we reviewed the wonderful flexibility of the telephone as a selling tool. Here's a summary of a few of the ways you can make your telephone work:

1. Generate more leads from advertising with an "800" number.
2. Put sign riders with your name and number on each "for sale" sign you place.
3. Circulate business cards with your name and number to everyone you meet.
4. Regularly contact past clients.
5. Check into expired listings.
6. Negotiate with "For Sale By Owner" listings.
7. Contact neighbors of a house you're listing.

To be at the top, you have to give your work the best you can. That means being creative, knowledgeable, helpful, and caring. The long hours you spend at the office sifting through records and organizing files may pale beside the thrill of selling. But the more and better you prepare, the quicker you'll be able to close your deals.

6. Selling Yourself Over the Phone

In the real estate business, everyone starts off at the same gate. You run the same course, have the same opportunities, and often work in the same neighborhoods. Some agents wind up owning half-million-dollar homes, while others struggle to pay their bills and quite often drift out of the business quickly.

Why do some people succeed and others merely get by? Because some people recognize that you don't just sell houses, you sell yourself.

The Prospect's Point of View

Before you pick up your phone to begin farming by phone, there's one thing you need to remember. It's a simple truth, but it's hard for some of us to put it into practice. In a nutshell, it's the fact that our prospects are not interested in us or what we want; they only care about what we can do for them.

Think about it for a moment. The key questions in

a prospect's mind are "Why is this person good for me? What can they do to help me?"

All too often, we approach a prospect by boasting about ourselves, our great sales record, all of the awards we've won, and the million-dollar deals.

Face it. Most of them couldn't care less. Sure, it helps build our credibility a little. But our impressive resume is not going to get us a single listing.

It's up to each one of us to prove to our prospects that we're genuinely concerned about them, about their finances, their needs, their problems, and their families.

As in a courtroom, the burden of proof is on us. We have to build a case to show that we can be of help to them, not by focusing the attention on us, but by focusing it on their needs.

To illustrate this point, here's an example of two ways to approach the same prospect.

Example 1:

> *"I'd like you to know that last week I sold the Smith home down your street for a great price!"*

Example 2:

> *"Just last week, I had the pleasure of helping the Smith family find a new home — you know, they just had a beautiful baby boy and they desperately needed an extra bedroom. The new home is just what they were looking for."*

After the first example, the prospect is thinking, "So what? You may think you're a hotshot . . . but you're not going to sell my home!"

After the second example, the line of thinking might go, "Here's a guy who really cares about his clients."

It's emotion that makes a person buy a home every time — no matter how good a deal he or she gets.

People aren't looking to buy things, they want what those things can do for them.

That means you have to focus on what owning a home does: improves their financial outlook, heightens their sense of security, gives them a feeling of achievement, makes them more accepted by others, bolsters their sense of self-worth, and increases their recognition. All of us share these motivations; ignoring them is perilous.

To be a success, it's critical that you learn to see things from your client's point of view. Then talk in terms of his wants, needs, and dreams.

The Magic Word — "You"

The one word that you never have to worry about using too often is "you."

In one 15-minute interview, insurance salesman Frank Bettger used "you" or "yours" 69 times.

Sounds repetitive and dull, doesn't it? But how often is someone so concerned about you and your needs that they'd be that interested?

Too many times, real estate professionals feel that their knowledge is superior to their clients'. And they don't hesitate to show that sense of superiority every chance they get. They do it not only in the words they choose, but in their voice and manner.

Arrogance is a character trait we see a lot of today. But humility, well, that seems to have gone the way of the covered wagon.

Many people don't realize you can be humble yet confident at the same time. Blending those traits will make people like you and will boost your commissions.

Next time you make a call, if the person asks, "What do you want to talk to me about?" try a one-word answer, "You." He or she is sure to say, "What about me?"

Maybe it's not the right moment to talk about how you can help him in real estate. Maybe you should talk about his job, his hobbies, or his son or daughter in college. Get to know people. Find out their needs. Then structure your approach.

If you never once refer to what you want — instead wrapping all your words around what the client wants — it may be impossible for him or her to say no.

Putting yourself in another person's shoes means you have to stop and think a minute; you have to try to see yourself through their eyes.

As a real estate professional, your job is to help people intelligently make a financial decision that probably involves their entire savings.

Help them see it that way, too.

What to Say

Research studies have shown that within the first four minutes of a face-to-face meeting, a person forms an opinion about you. Moreover, over half of that opinion is based on nonverbal communication — the way you stand, the look in your eye, whether you're fidgeting, your hairstyle, and the type of clothes you're wearing.

Over the phone, instead of four minutes you have just 15 seconds to make an impression. And 100% of that impression hinges on how you come across verbally.

Sometimes it's probably a plus that you're limited to sounds passing over the telephone wire. Other times, it puts you in a negative position.

Create Warmth

Either way, you compensate for the lack of touch, eye contact, gestures, and movements — the subtle physical expressions that often reveal the way we really feel through our inner voice.

Some of us, of course, are more adept at concealing our emotions. But some studies hint that just by listening to our voices, people can tell with 90% accuracy whether we feel positive or negative toward them.

When you make a call, the person on the other end also is instantly aware of how you feel about yourself, and they respond accordingly. Think of all the times you've picked up the phone and as soon as the other person said, "Hello," you knew there was a problem.

How many times have you had a salesperson call you on the phone and all you heard in his voice was the desire to make a pitch?

How many times have you hung up, thinking, "What a pushy person that was on the other end of the line!"?

It doesn't have to be that way.

If we can use our voices to put people off, we can also use them to draw people to us. From the very beginning of the call, you have the chance to create a sense of friendship and warmth, setting the stage for your entire relationship with that client.

It's also in those critical first 15 seconds that you win or lose control of the conversation.

Assume Control

For example, if you run into someone who responds to your offer for a free home market evaluation with, "I'm not going to sell my home. Who do you think you are, bothering me like this? I'm a busy person. I don't have time for people like you."

If you respond, "I'm sorry I bothered you," and hang up, you've lost control and given up too soon.

On the other hand, if you counter with a response such as, "I appreciate the fact that you're a busy person. I can see by the way you take care of your home that you use your time wisely. That's why you especially might be interested in finding out what all those hours you've put into your home are worth. In the long run, it could save you time and money."

Now the ball is back in your court and you're ready to go with it.

There is one way you can lose control and credibility in about 10 seconds. It's a path that inexperienced salespeople sometimes follow.

At first glance, it may seem the route of least resistance. But watch out, because all you're doing is digging yourself a hole.

It happens when you dial a number, pleasantly greet the person who answers, then right off the top utter those infamous words, "Do you want to sell your house?"

Sales is a matter of friendly persuasion. Here there has been no persuasion at all, just a black-and white question about a situation your prospect may not even have contemplated.

Do yourself a favor and tell yourself you'll never start off a call this way. Give people a reason to buy or a reason to list. Guide them to a decision and help them rationalize the decision, but always let them think they're making the decision for themselves.

You're still in control, but they have the satisfaction of coming to their own conclusions. It's the only way to work.

Words Do Matter

Every day, each of us speaks thousands of words, usually rattling off whatever comes into our heads.

But look at the difference the way we say things can make. For example, when showing a house to a prospective buyer, I could say, "Look at the lovely garden out back." Or I could say, "Just imagine the colorful azaleas and roses you'll have blooming here this summer."

The first is a bland general statement; the second plucks at the prospect's imagination, conjuring up warm pictures — psychologically, it also hints at ownership. In sales especially, you need to think before you speak. And there are certain words you can use that work better than others.

Behind all this, of course, is the fact that the words we choose don't just fall flat on our listener's ears. Instead they draw pictures, touch emotions, and inspire action.

What a difference it would have made in the Gettysburg Address if Abraham Lincoln had started off, "87 years ago," instead of the famous "Four score and seven years ago."

Here are a few rules of thumb to use in selecting your words and putting together your sentences.

Use Active Words

Always try to use active words instead of passive ones. It's a simple trick that gives you greater strength verbally.

For example, don't say, "The letter will be mailed today." It's better to say, "I'll personally drop it in the mailbox this afternoon."

Using "will be" shrugs off responsibility for mailing it, raising a question in the listener's mind as to who will do it. The other way is much clearer. Here are some more examples:

> *"A park is being built up the street."*
> *"The County Parks Department is building a park up the street."*

> *"You'll only be able to receive this offer for a limited time."*
> *"This offer is good only until the end of the month."*

> *"The living room could always be re-painted."*
> *"You could always repaint the living room."*

Avoid Weak Words

Using weak words, especially over the phone, makes you appear a weaker personality to your listener.

Always avoid what some of us call "weasel words": "if," "if you like," "if I may," "might," "possibly," "rather," "very," "little."

Instead, give an impression of strength. However, although you want to appear confident and informed, don't go overboard. Make sure your words are warm and clear, painting desirable pictures in the listener's mind.

Appeal to the Senses

Words that appeal to the senses are good. For example: "peace," "tranquility," "spacious," "fragrant," "cozy," and "comfortable." Think about these words especially when you're describing property. If someone starts talking to you about a "starter home," what do you conjure up? Probably a two bedroom cracker box, with a pint-sized yard, maybe one tree, and on a busy street. Not very appealing, is it?

Describe the same property as a picturesque dollhouse or charming country cottage, and watch your phone start to ring.

Speak in a Conversational Tone

When we talk, no matter how much preparation has gone into our conversation, it's important that our speech sound natural. All too often, when you pick up the phone and a salesperson is on the other end, you can tell in a second that his or her speech is canned.

Colorful, descriptive words are good; so are personal words that draw someone into a conversation. Phrases like "isn't it?" "wouldn't it?" and "couldn't it?" can work wonders by getting your listener personally involved.

False compliments are out. Using them only tells the listener that you're insincere and you can't be trusted.

Another important point to remember is to focus all of your remarks on the listener. Avoid anything that starts with: "Don't you know..." or "Let me tell you about . . ." or "My friend . . ." Using that kind of language subtly tells the listener that your attention isn't really on him or her, but on yourself and what you can get out of them. It's a form of put-down and that's something not many people will put up with. At least not from you.

Weed Out the Negatives

To present a more positive image, some people recommend weeding all the "little negatives" out of your speech. To a prospective client, it's important that you show yourself in a positive light, as someone who is free of a critical spirit and who looks on the bright side of things.

Now that doesn't mean you're Pollyannish or too cheerful. If someone's having problems, empathize with them. But overall, don't let it seem that you're critical or judgmental. People don't like that.

That's something many of us do subconsciously. You have to work at catching yourself. But it's worth it. Remember what your mother used to say, "If you can't say something good about someone, don't say anything at all." That's good advice for salespeople, too.

There are certain words that are negatives. Words like "buy" and "sell." People, as we've all been told before, don't like to *buy* houses, they like to *own* homes.

Look at the difference in these statements:

"I can help you sell your home."
"I can help you find a new owner for your home."

The first statement is weighty with the chore of selling, part of which falls on the owner listing the property, or so it appears from the sentence.

The second statement is more pleasing to the ear and to the imagination. Now we're not looking for a buyer; we're trying to find a new owner. The seller is put in the light of wanting to do something good for his or her home, not the mercenary position of simply wanting to sell.

These differences are quite subtle and some of you may be thinking it's making a mountain out of a molehill. But believe me, the words we choose reveal a lot about how we feel inside. They deserve our attention.

BAD WORDS	GOOD WORDS
Cost	Value
Price	Worth
Down Payment	Initial Investment
Buy	Belongs
Purchase	Own
Contract	Assurance
Decision	Choose
Difficult	Easy
Drawbacks	Results
Liability	Appreciate
Expensive	Valuable
	Proven
	Proud
	New
	Trust
	Comfort
	Fun
	Profit
	Save
	YOU

Keep It Simple

In the words and phrases you choose, keep it simple. For you, things like wraparound mortgages, trust deeds, title insurance, and disclosure statements may be old hat. But not to the person you're talking to.

You don't have to patronize someone or talk down to them, but you do have to make yourself understood without putting them in the humiliating position of asking, "Could you explain that, please?"

Rather than ask, most people will hang up and spare themselves the embarrassment.

Also, never follow up a statement with the question, "Do you understand?" Who's going to admit they don't? By using that kind of language, you're giving yourself an air of superiority — an impression you want to avoid at all costs.

Never feel bad about keeping things simple and clear. That's one of the hallmarks of genius. If you read the speeches of Abraham Lincoln or the letters of Thomas Jefferson or a biography of Albert Einstein, you'll see that the greatest among us have always had the ability to relate to everybody.

When we use fancy words, the only people we're impressing are ourselves.

But our prospects are the ones who count.

What's in a Name?

Everyone's name is important to them, even if they don't like it. Using someone's name in conversation tells them that we respect them as an individual — that we think of them as someone we value.

You'll kill a call in the first few seconds if you

don't start off with a name. That shows a lack of professionalism.

One tip for any call you make is to use the person's name as much as possible, without going overboard.

If a name is extremely unusual, you may want to ask about it in the course of the conversation. There could be an interesting story behind it.

Once you meet the person, make an effort to connect the name and the face. If you have to, use mental tricks to trigger your memory. Sometimes it helps to associate the name with an object or make up a sentence with it.

For example, "Mr. and Mrs. Kingman live next to the Castles on 48th Street." Kings and Castles — they go together, don't they?

Using names in conversations also helps remind you that your farm is made up of real people, people with names and faces, with individual needs and dreams, people who deserve your personal attention.

Making the Right Offer

When your phone rings, there's a reason. If a friend keeps chatting on and on, finally we'll say, "What did you want?"

The same thing applies to calls you make. You have to have a reason for calling every home you dial. And it should be a good reason.

If, like an inexperienced agent, you keep talking without really saying anything, chances are you'll lose that appointment.

So approach farming by phone the way you'd approach sending a letter or making a personal visit — have a plan. In devising your plan, it's best to use everything you know about that person or his or her home. By now, you've already driven through your farm.

You should have an idea of their income level, the style of home they seem to like, whether they're big on gardens, and what kind of car they drive.

All those notes should be on your Manual Farm Form before you ever sit down to call. When you do call, what should you say?

Having the right offer, or proposition, is critical to your success. Some of the offers that work well in farming by mail are: free home market evaluations, Home-Seller's Kits, open house invitations, free gifts, and For-Sale-By-Owner Kits.

Over the phone, however, you can tailor each offer more personally. Perhaps you have buyers looking for a ranch home in the Whispering Pines area of your city. Checking in your reverse directory, you find the names and phone numbers of everyone who has a shingled ranch in that area.

Your call might go something like this:

Realtor: Good evening, Mr. Bernard. This is Greg Jones with Star Realty here in Pottstown. Do you have a minute to talk?

Prospect: Well, just a minute.

Realtor: Mr. Bernard, I was wondering if you could help me. You see, I'm trying to help a nice young couple, Linda and Edward Smith. Edward is an engineer for Hughes Aircraft, and Linda is a paralegal. Edward has just been transferred to this area from Tucson, and they're very concerned about finding a home in a good school district for their two wonderful children. Knowing that the schools in Whispering Pines are among the best in the city, they've decided to look only in your area. I was wondering...do you know anyone who might be thinking about selling? Maybe one of your friends or neighbors?

From a call that begins like this, a realtor may have the good fortune to find someone who's really thinking of selling their home. If he doesn't, chances are that from 15 or 20 calls, he'll at least get the names of four or five people who have mentioned selling.

But even if he doesn't get any names, he's made an impression on Mr. Bernard — an impression of someone who gives personal attention to each of his clients. He also shows he's not afraid to take risks.

Compare his approach to the pushy agent who calls and right after introducing himself says, "We have several people interested in buying in this neighborhood. May we show your property?"

To the listener, that's a slap in the face. He'll probably be thinking, "Who is this guy anyway? My house isn't for sale. Who does he think he is?"

In dreaming up offers, be as imaginative and creative as you can. Just be sure that each one has substance.

Home Protection — Not long ago, there was a terrible tragedy in a neighborhood nearby, when the killer nicknamed the Night Stalker broke into a home in the middle of the night and murdered a woman's husband.

The next day, enterprising security companies were knocking on doors and ringing up a lot of sales. If they had thought of it, realtors could've offered a Home-Protection Kit, with leaflets, coupons, and the names and addresses of all the local security companies.

Pulling the kit together would've taken a few days. By enlisting the help of the companies themselves or the local police department, the costs would've been minimal.

Then all they would have had to do is call each

home in the area, talk a little about the tragedy and how it could have been prevented, and then mention the kit they were offering.

Again, with a call like this, you're painting a picture of yourself as a caring, creative real estate agent. On the kit, of course, the agent's name and telephone number would be prominently displayed.

Income Property — Perhaps your farm is in an affluent area, where homeowners would be interested in owning rental or income properties. For example, if you have a nice four-plex on the market, with good financing, why not call a few people to see if they're interested?

Financing — Checking the records, you know that the turnover in your farm is low and that many homeowners bought when mortgage rates were around 13%. On your Manual Farm Form, you have the date each home was purchased. If someone bought when rates were up, why not call and see if they'd be interested in owning a larger home for the same monthly payment? Maybe there's one on the market just three blocks away.

Renters — By driving around, you've spotted a courtyard of Spanish bungalows you know are rental properties. Judging the local rental market, you'd guess each tenant is paying $700 a month. For that same amount, they could own a home. Since renters don't always realize the tax and other advantages of home ownership, why don't you call and tell them?

Prospect Interest — Several years back, a friend spotted a house she fell in love with. It had gingerbread trim, a massive stone fireplace, and walls of windows overlooking a mountain canyon.

She insisted the agent contact the owner to see if he was willing to sell. To her surprise, he didn't say no. Instead, he promised to think about it.

Remember, most houses change hands every five years. If your client suffers from love at first glance, don't hesitate to follow it up. The owner might not be willing to sell now; but four years down the road, your client may still be interested, even if he or she has bought another home.

Free Home Evaluations — Offering a free home evaluation can work well if someone just finished building a new garage, adding on some extra bedrooms, or putting in a pool. Every homeowner likes to know how smart they are to have increased the value of their home.

As you can see from all these examples, farming by phone can be more personal and timely than farming by mail. And the more personal you are, the greater the likelihood you'll have of developing a relationship and eventually getting a customer.

Can Telephoning Work for You?

For anyone in sales, the telephone can make their work more efficient and more effective. Remember, people are selling everything from artistic masterpieces to computer bits over the phone lines.

Being a good salesperson usually isn't a natural gift; you have to cultivate the right skills. Doing so takes time and effort.

If you read the biographies of this country's greatest salespeople, you'll see that many of them started out with two left feet, one of them in their mouth.

Years ago, Lee Iacocca launched his career as a fumbling sales representative. In his autobiography, *Iacocca,* the plain-speaking and straight-shooting Chrysler Corporation chairman remembers, "Some people think that good salesmen are born and not made. But I had no natural talent. Most of my colleagues were a lot more relaxed and outgoing than I was.

"For the first year or two, I was theoretical and stilted. Eventually I got some experience under my belt and started to improve. Once I had mastered the facts, I worked on how to present them. Before long, people started listening to me."

If Lee Iacocca can do it, so can you, if you're willing to make a personal commitment to succeed. In this generation, commitment is what separates the winners from the losers.

Summary

In today's competitive market, selling yourself is a critical element of your success. It begins with the basics: choosing the right words, and saying them the right way.

As a real estate agent, on every call your first job is to plant the seeds that open the door to an interview. You do that by drawing mental pictures with your words.

Some words are cozy and comfortable; others are harsh and unforgiving. Learn to turn around the bad words with good words, and see how the image you send over the phone changes for the better.

When you call, uppermost in the prospect's mind is the thought, "What can this person do for me?"

From the beginning, direct every ounce of persuasion to letting the prospect know you genuinely care about him or her. Don't focus the spotlight on yourself; let it shine on the person you're talking to. Make him or her feel important. One way to do that is by using the person's name throughout your conversation.

You have just 15 seconds to buy the time you need to complete the call. Here you're not pitching an interview, you're just trying to sell the call.

Once it's sold, have a solid and simple offer ready. Know as much as you can about the person you're talking to, and use that knowledge in your presentation. Whatever you do, make an offer that has substance. Otherwise, you're wasting their time and your own.

With the phone, you can be wonderfully versatile in your approach. It should be personal, topical, and warm. Remember, the one word you can never wear out is *you*.

7. Tips on Telephoning

Like every other form of communication, telephoning has, over the years, developed its own rules of etiquette.

Hear any one of these phrases and you'd know in a second it had to do with the phone: "Call me back," "Hold on," "Just a minute, please," "Could I take a message?" and "All our representatives are busy now. Please stay on the line and we'll be with you in a moment."

In this chapter, we're going to look at some of the courtesies involved in telephoning, as well as ways you can develop your voice to make a more effective presentation.

Where You Are

The surroundings that you call from can make a big difference in your mood.

If your desk is one of 15 crammed into a small, high-ceiling, noisy room with elevator music playing in the background, consider calling from your home.

Distractions and interruptions can't disturb you during your calls — not if you're going to do a good job of listening to what a prospect is saying, interpreting it, and working out your response.

If you are calling from home, make sure you don't have any unusual background noises, such as children playing or a vacuum cleaner running. Not only will these distract you, they'll also distract the person you're talking to.

As a general rule, call from a comfortable and pleasant environment, a place where you feel relaxed. Keep your farm files nearby, and be sure your desk top has plenty of room for spreading out papers and taking notes.

When to Call

You can find all kinds of schedules of the best time to call people in different occupations. They're interesting, but not for you.

When farming by phone, you're calling people at their homes. The Direct Marketing Association's *Guidelines for Ethical Business Practices* say that all telephone contacts should be made during reasonable hours. Generally, that's from 9 a.m. to 9 p.m.

Time of Day

To reach people who work, it's best to call during dinnertime, anywhere from 5 p.m. to 8 p.m. Then you have a good chance of catching them between getting home from work and taking off for a meeting or social engagement.

Although you might think people don't like to be disturbed during these hours, you'd be surprised.

With the huge variations in when we eat our

meals and the short amount of time those meals usually take, I hardly ever interrupt anyone in the middle of their dinner. If I do, I take just a moment to set up a time to call back.

If your plan is to reach people who don't work, the best time to call is between 9 a.m. and 10 a.m. By then, the children are off to school and the parent at home is usually picking up the house, getting ready to start the day.

Afternoons are generally a dead time to call, unless you want to reach retired people.

Days of the Week

As for the days of the week, avoid Friday. By then, most people's minds are wandering far from business matters.

During the week, I call any day, Monday through Thursday. Saturday morning is also a good time to find people at home (usually doing chores and maybe muttering to themselves about all the repair bills). On Sundays, let people sleep in or go to church. You can then phone anytime from 1 p.m. to 8 p.m.

When you call, if no one answers or if the line's busy, jot a note down on their farm index card — "NH" for not home and "B" for busy are fine. If it is busy, try back again in 15 minutes. If they're not home, plan to make another call the next night.

Whatever you do, don't give up after one or two attempts. You should make about six attempts to reach each individual. If they are hard to find at home, chances are that's true for every other agent who calls them.

So your persistence in phoning can pay off.

Courtesy Counts

Erastus Wiman once said, "Nothing is ever lost by courtesy. It is the cheapest of the pleasures, costs nothing, and conveys much. It pleases him who gives and him who receives, and thus, like mercy, is twice blessed."

It's true that it makes you feel good to be nice to people. And a reputation for kindness never hurt anybody.

When it comes to our manners over the phone, sometimes I think we carry them over from our teenage years.

Sometimes I've been put on hold for more than 10 minutes. Even with music on the line, I'm still fuming by the time they answer.

Or I've been talking to people who carried on two conversations at once — one with me, the other with someone in the room with them. Or I've had people washing dishes as I talked, with running water drowning out every other word.

Common courtesies we would never overlook in person seem to easily slip by the wayside over the phone.

What kind of person do you like to talk to over the phone?

Is it someone who:

Puts you on hold	*or*	*Gives you full attention*
Chews gum or eats candy in your ear	*or*	*Talks clearly*
Talks above your head	*or*	*Speaks simply*
Puts you down	*or*	*Builds you up*

Has a chill in his or her voice	*or*	*Speaks warmly*
Talks to someone in the background	*or*	*Focuses only on you*
Doesn't answer your questions	*or*	*Gives you clear answers*
Interrupts you or finishes your sentences	*or*	*Lets you speak your mind*
Talks about himself	*or*	*Talks about you*

That's quite a lengthy list, covering a lot of ground. But it's a good synopsis of things to avoid on the phone. And it should help you think more about treating people the way you would like to be treated.

Never Use "Hold" Buttons

Every time you put a caller on hold, you're subconsciously telling them, "The other person who's calling is more important than you are." Only in extreme emergencies should you ever use the hold button.

If you find that you have to, don't stay away longer than 15 seconds.

When you come back on the line, don't dismiss the interruption with a curt "Sorry to keep you waiting."

Instead give a full apology: "I'm sorry, Mr. Smith. Thank you for waiting."

It may also be a good idea to briefly summarize where you left off. That way, you can recreate the mood of the moment, which may have shifted when you put the call on hold.

Use Prospect's Name Frequently

William Shakespeare's famous line, "A rose by any other name would smell as sweet" does not apply to people. As we know, a person's name is important to them. If you're calling someone you've never met, don't start off on the wrong foot by using their first name.

Nowadays people are getting more casual, and using first names is becoming a way of doing business. People seem to think it makes them appear more friendly.

If you believe that, read Ann Landers. You'll see a number of letters from people who take offense at a stranger calling them Marie or George instead of Mrs. Berrenger or Mr. Husman.

They may not have the courage to tell you over the phone that they think you're being rude, but don't expect them to agree to an appointment.

Use "Please" and "Thank-You"

Some things never go out of style and words like "please" and "thank-you" are among them.

It's flattering when the people we're talking to use them, and judicious flattery is something we all enjoy.

Know When to Stop Talking

A salesperson can never know too much, but he or she can talk too much. And many do.

Knowing when to keep your mouth shut is an ability that doesn't come naturally. All of us like to hear ourselves talk, so why wouldn't other people, too?

Well, they like to hear themselves talk, but not you. The more you talk, especially if you have nothing to say, the more likely you'll lose that prospect.

Letting someone talk is more than a measure of politeness; it's a sign that what they have to say is important to you.

Don't you want your clients to feel that way?

Never Interrupt or Finish Someone's Sentences

Here again, you're putting yourself in the driver's seat. By interrupting, you're saying, "That thought isn't important. Listen to me, you turkey."

When you finish a sentence for someone, you're telling them that you already know what they want to say, that your mind works quicker than theirs does, and that they should hurry up with their speech.

Pay Attention

One of the discourtesies many of us show our families every day is not focusing on what they're saying to us.

Sometimes you can hide it, but not over the phone.

Your prospects need to sense that their thoughts and feelings are important to you. And if you miss a crucial word or ask someone to repeat something, you've lost whatever trust you're trying to build.

Pay attention. It's worth it to you.

Never Argue

Later you'll see how to twist an objection around into an advantage. But for now, remember never to argue with a prospective client. It's okay to have differences, but always give the client's viewpoint a little credit. When you argue or have an opinion you refuse to soften, you're adding a tone and implications that are not healthy for your relationship. If you have a quick temper, this is something you may have to work on. But engrave this rule in stone: *Never argue with a prospect or client.*

Keep It Short and Simple

Over the phone, you usually have three to four minutes to talk to your prospect. If you talk any longer, people lose concentration.

Three or four minutes may not sound like a lot, but you can pack a lot of powerful words into that time slot. The key is planning what you're going to say, knowing appropriate responses, and keeping the conversation on track.

You'll find that you can still be friendly, while avoiding being long-winded.

Never Hang Up First

This adage should go on the stone, next to "Never argue." The reason for it is simple: Think of all the times you started screaming someone's name into the phone after you said good-bye, because you had one more thought.

More often than not, they'd probably already hung up.

Hanging up last, after you hear the other receiver placed back into its cradle, is another courtesy that tells your listener he or she is important to you.

Watch Your Favorite Words

On a plane not long ago, I started counting the number of times one of the flight attendants said, "Sure."
"I'd like a Coke." "Sure."
"Do you have any lemon?" "Sure."
"What about a glass of milk?" "Sure."
She must have used the word 50 times in five minutes. I stopped listening to whatever she was saying, because I was so engrossed in counting the number of times she used "sure."

Another phrase we tend to repeat time and time again is the infamous "you know." That can slip in almost anywhere.

If you have a favorite phrase or word, be careful not to use it too often. If you do, it sounds like your mind is someplace else while you're talking.

If You Call at a Bad Time, Reschedule the Call

There are certain days and moments when the ringing of the phone is an unwelcome intrusion. Don't give up easily; but if you sense this definitely is not the time to talk, schedule a time to call back. By doing so, you'll be calling by invitation. And you're almost sure to get the person to listen to what you have to say, because they'll feel bad about cutting you off the first time.

Remember, being courteous is an easy way to prove that people are important to you.

Soften Your Words

Before we move on, here are a few word tricks to make you sound more pleasing over the phone:

Don't Say This:	***Say This:***
Hold on.	*Just a moment, please.*
We must have . . .	*May we have . . .?*
You ought to . . .	*Perhaps you could . . .*
Sorry to keep you waiting.	*Thank-you for waiting.*
Good-bye.	*Thank-you for your time.*
Who's calling?	*May I ask your name, please?*
What's your name?	*And your name is?*

Secret of Success

When you're selling over the phone, the secret to success is using your voice to create an image of self-confidence, intelligence, and caring.

So often salespeople on the phone sound just alike: bored with their jobs, going through the motions, and following their directions step-by-step.

That's not exactly the way to make people think you're inspired, creative, and good at what you do.

Your voice is an instrument that you can use to play a humdrum, ordinary tune, or you can fill it with valleys and peaks.

Over the phone, a good sales voice is:

- Clear
- Well paced
- Friendly
- Sincere
- Confident
- Relaxed
- Cheerful

Your phone manner should be professional and courteous, but always persuasive.

Talking over the phone is not the same as talking to someone in person. Because they can't see the movements of your hands or the expressions on your face, your voice has to become a portrait of your personality. Your voice has to make gestures, carry your facial expressions, and tease out responses.

It has to be full of lightness and darkness, softness and determination, playfulness and factualness, smoothness and rhythm. In other words, your voice has to convey the real you.

Here are some tips on tuning up your voice.

Put a Smile in Your Voice

Before you make a call, take a moment and pause. Then smile — big. Putting a smile on your face puts a smile in your voice. That's the best way to come across sounding pleasant, lively, enthusiastic, and expectant. Don't forget to keep smiling throughout the call.

In addition to a smile, good intonations can make a world of difference in how you sound. They not only add interest and sparkle to your voice, they also help get across your meaning.

Here's a simple example:

"Just a moment." (The voice falls at the end.)
"Just a moment." (The voice rises at the end.)

We have the same words, only said two different ways.

With the first example, there's the unconscious feeling that you're bothering the person talking, that it's a chore to do whatever you've asked them.

With the second example, the person talking sounds eager, warm, and pleased to help. Which impression would you rather create?

Slow Down Your Speech

If you talk too quickly over the phone, your words can run together and the listener has a hard time understanding you.

On the other hand, if you talk too slowly, the listener's hanging on the other end, frustrated and wondering, "Why doesn't this slowpoke hurry up?"

The pace at which you speak is more important over the phone than it is in person. If you're talking too fast or too slow, the poor pacing is much more pronounced.

At the beginning of a call, you should talk a little slower than you normally do. Experts say 140 to 150 words a minute is ideal.

Talking more slowly helps the person on the other end concentrate better and understand what you're saying.

Lower Your Voice Pitch

Some of us have high-pitched voices; others have low-pitched voices.

Actress Katharine Hepburn used to have a terrible time trying to control her voice. Whenever she became excited, it would run up very high, hitting jarring and displeasing notes.

With the help of a voice coach, through singing, she learned to control it and keep it on pitch.

In direct-response broadcast advertising, deep male voices are almost always used, primarily because they add an air of authority and believability.

You don't have to go so far as to mimic their deep voices, but remember that the deeper your voice, the more confident and knowledgeable you sound.

Speak Directly into the Phone

A simple trick, but one we sometimes forget, is this: Don't let the receiver hang below your mouth. Keep it about a half inch directly in front of your lips and talk straight into it. It's the only way to make sure your voice is clear.

Listen to Your Own Voice

How does your own voice sound? Does it sound confident? Caring? Sincere? Natural? In the next chapter, we're going to discuss using a cassette player to practice your scripts for the phone. When you do, you might be surprised at the quality of your voice.

How many times have you heard a voice that you didn't quite recognize as your own?

That's because when you talk, the sound comes back to you through the vibrations of your bones. You don't hear yourself the way the rest of the world does. To them, the sound is carried into their eardrums through the air.

Improving the quality of our voices is something we all can do.

The first step is to ask someone objective to evaluate it. Does it sometimes sound tinny? Or abrasive? Harsh? Grating? Is there enough resonance in it?

When you're checking your voice, see if you have a

problem with sloppy pronunciation, misplaced breathing, a monotonous tone, or maybe you drop the end of every sentence. Those problems are common and they're easily corrected. All you have to do is practice.

Enunciate Clearly

The English language is full of words that are hard to pronounce. When you string them together, they can be almost impossible to say.

Over the phone, if you mush your words, the listener won't understand you. You have to articulate each and every sound clearly. You'll come across better and you'll spare people the embarrassment of asking you to repeat something.

The only way to practice enunciation is in front of a mirror. See if you can read your lips while you talk. Some of us, like me, are lazy and we tend to move our lips as little as possible while we're speaking. As a result, our words are muddled.

Sounds that are especially difficult are "s," "t," "d," "p," and "b."

For starters, why don't you practice reading the following paragraphs in front of your mirror?

When the snow falls, the sleighs glide across the glen, their slick blades skimming over the shiny surface of the ice. A popular pastime for people of all ages, sleighing stirs a sense of nostalgia.

Fur-lined coats, steaming cups of coffee, the chirping of birds, the glistening patches of snow . . . all make beautiful memories.

Today in the roofed and covered rinks where children on skates practice their pirouettes, there is no cool breeze blowing through their hair or chill nipping at their noses. Something good is gone.

When you have this down pat, you should be able to clearly read your lips in front of the mirror while you're saying every word.

Voice Matching

One of the tricks phone pros use is to match their voice to the person they're calling. If the other voice is soft, they soften theirs. If it's brusque and businesslike, they turn into Mr. or Ms. Efficiency.

Matching voices helps create an aura of understanding and mutuality that can never hurt you. After all, we all tend to be drawn to people who are like us.

Another hint is to echo back to people the same words they're using when talking to you. This, too, helps build a sense of trust.

For example, if someone says, "I'm not sure we're interested in looking at any houses."

Your response should be something like, "But if you look at these houses, I think you'll find . . ."

Instead of the word "look," you could've used "see" or "visit." But each word is slightly different, and by using "look," you're showing that the two of you are on the same wavelength.

Remember, with your voice, you're creating a portrait of your personality in sound. Fill it in with the depths of blue, the sunniness of yellow, the passion of red, the soothing shades of green, the shadows of black and brown, and the delicacy of pink.

And, most of all, make your voice reflect the real you.

Summary

Miss Manners' amusing approach to etiquette hides in it a gem of truth: The little ways we treat people often make a big difference. Making sure we're kind and polite is often even more important on the phone than it is in person.

Before you begin farming by phone, make sure you're in a comfortable, pleasant environment, where you feel relaxed and there are no background noises to divert you.

When considering the times to schedule your calls, make them during the evenings Monday through Thursday, on Saturday morning, or on Sunday afternoon.

Then polish up your manners. Over the phone, courtesy requires that you *never* do the following:

- Put a prospect on hold
- Interrupt or finish a prospect's sentence
- Let your mind wander
- Argue with a prospect
- Be long winded
- Hang up first

With your voice, you're creating a portrait of yourself in sound. You want that picture to be cheerful, relaxed, confident, sincere, clear, and pleasing to the ear.

If you listen to your voice and you're not happy with it, ask someone objective to help you. Work out the kinks by practicing in front of a mirror.

Every good actress or actor knows that you can smooth away a heavy accent, find a better pace, add emotion and warmth, or learn to pick up and bounce back the voice of the person you're talking to. All it takes is practice.

Finally, the voice with a smile in it is the voice that wins. To have a smile in your voice, first put one on your face. See how much better it makes you feel.

8. The Farm Call Script

Some of you may be frightened by the word "script." Don't be. We're not talking about a canned spiel that you mechanically deliver. What we mean is a format that enables you to strike up a conversation with a clear purpose, direction, flexibility, and consistency.

Think of it as your path to a goal. In this case, the goal is setting up an appointment. By having a road map, you'll spare yourself many detours and distractions.

In this business, you not only have to know what you want. You have to know how you're going to get there, too.

What a Script Can Do for You

As we've said before, over the phone, you have the opportunity to personally tailor every effort to suit your prospects.

Looking at your farm, if your farm full of young families, structure the script around the ease of owning a larger home. If it's in a wealthy area, plug the advantages of income property. Make your script fit your clients' needs, and you'll go a lot further a lot faster.

Using a script is helpful because it:

Gives You a Plan of Action

Never again do you have to start off a call with "Do you want to sell your home?" By plotting a creative, innovative strategy, you can write scripts that make people want to meet you — not because you're so brilliant, but because you can help them and you let them know it.

It takes a little time and thinking; but doesn't anything in life that's worthwhile?

Helps You Overcome Objections

You can know in advance 60% of what will be said during any given conversation, if you have a script.

The other 40% may be up for grabs, but it's highly unlikely anyone is going to throw you a curve ball.

After a few sessions of farming by phone, you'll see the same kinds of objections and responses cropping up over and over again.

With a script, you'll know exactly the approach you want to use in overcoming each of these objections. You'll be able to anticipate any question you might be asked, come up with alternatives, and figure out how you're going to answer — all before you ever dial one number.

You'll be surprised at how that kind of thorough preparation helps you feel more confident and self-assured.

Makes Your Presentation Consistent

Whenever we make a call, there's the danger that we'll get off track. Maybe someone starts talking about their problems with a neighbor, a disagreement with their husband or wife, or a sickness they've recently suffered.

That may sound farfetched, but there are some people in this world who have no one to really talk to. Sometimes an anonymous voice is a good way for them to let off steam.

When that happens, have empathy for them. But don't let them wander too far off base.

Having a script will help you control someone who's rambling, because you'll know exactly where you want the conversation to go next.

A word of warning: Sometimes it's good just to let people talk. By listening to their troubles, you lend a sympathetic ear that they'll remember. So be sensitive to each situation. Remember, you are trying to be their friend.

Provides Logical Organization

When you talk, how often do your thoughts follow each other logically?

Probably not as often as you'd like to think.

All of us tend to believe we're making perfect sense and that anyone could understand our reasoning. But count all the times you had to go over and over something, trying to get someone else to understand. Finally, you hit on one analogy or expression that clarified the whole thing.

When you're farming by phone, you don't have time to experiment with logic. You've got to know, before the other person ever answers, what the most reasonable and sound approach is that you can take. Don't forget, you're taking up the friendly art of persuasion. That means you have to build your case. You have to lead someone along, giving them reasons to agree with you — until you come to the clincher, asking for an appointment.

All of us like to think we're making our own decisions about whether we want to follow something through. You have to know how to persuade people that that's exactly what they're doing.

Your job is to make people see a need to have you help them. You can't expect them to know they have that need before you call. Telling them outright isn't going to do the trick. Be a gentle persuader, and you can have it all.

Stresses Benefits over Features

This is a phrase that sales experts love to use. It's a little confusing, but all it means is to show people how what you do can make their lives better.

In other words, when you're selling someone a house, you're not selling a house on a piece of land.

Maybe you're selling them the swimming pool, with the house thrown in. Or the shade trees that grace the spacious backyard. Or the charming wood trim that gives the interior character.

People don't buy houses, they own homes — homes that express who and what they are.

In the middle of a conversation, with the seconds ticking away, it's tough not to be practical and toss out the facts. Having a script helps you have the mental pictures ready. You won't have to think twice about how to separate benefits from features, because your entire strategy and the tack you'll take after every remark is laying right there before your eyes.

Yields Better Results

If an inexperienced salesperson can get one or two appointments out of every 20 calls, and if the experienced salesperson can get one appointment out of every three or four calls, then obviously you learn by experience.

There is a science to trying to set up real estate appointments over the phone. Believe me, it's not just a matter of having a pleasing personality.

That's why the first year or so in any sales job is often a real struggle. You haven't keyed in yet on the little things you can do that make a huge difference in your commissions.

It's a thrill to put into practice what you learn, and you're fortunate because you can measure the results.

Through your Call Response Tally, evaluating your performance at the end of every month and again at the end of every year, you have the opportunity to grow every day.

You may be good now, but by the time you finish this book, you'll be even better.

In essence, a script helps you organize your information, allowing you to weed out extraneous facts and figures. It helps you clarify where you want the conversation to go and what you want it to focus on.

To the person you're talking to, a script helps you sound smoother and more together. The answers to their questions are nearby, and whatever objection they raise, you know immediately how you want to handle it.

With so much help at your fingertips, you'll find your self-confidence higher than it's ever been before. But remember, your script is never truly finished.

Every script you write has to stand the test of time.

If it's not working as well as you'd like, be willing to change it. Fix the words. Write a new offer. Make it more to the point. Weave in something that just happened.

Remember the Boy Scouts' motto? *Be prepared.* Make that your motto, too.

Script Formats That Work

With companies using telemarketing so many ways, it shouldn't come as a surprise that you can choose what type of script you want to use.

Basically there are four kinds of scripts from which to choose:

Word-for-Word Scripts — Like a machine, the person making the call sticks to every line they read. Usually this rigid structure is only appropriate when you're dealing with a highly technical product; or legal requirements may dictate a by-the-book approach.

Logical Flow Scripts — Here some of the script is quoted word for word. But in other sections, the salesperson picks and chooses what he or she says. Maybe you use the scripted lines at the beginning, introducing a product or service. But then you move right on into a more personal and persuasive appeal.

Prompt Scripts — With these, you have the facts at your fingertips. They're helpful if you expect questions that need explicit answers, but you don't want a rigid structure.

Call Outline Scripts — This book will focus on this one, because this is the type of script we use for farming. Here you follow a general outline, with important points noted for you to refer to. Built into the script, there's room for lots of personal interaction, so you and your prospects can get to know each other. In telemarketing lingo, this script is a *rapport builder.* To you, just think of it as a way of making friends.

Script a Conversation

When you think of a script, don't think about it as a list of questions you absolutely must get through, or as a series of points that you'll be slighting if you don't finish them.

Your script is only meant to give you a snappy opening, quick responses, and to spark a conversation.

It's a plan to get to know someone, to zero in on their needs and their dreams, so you can figure out the best way to help achieve them.

That's why a lot of fluffy phrases or high-talking words don't belong there. Keep it simple, person-to-person, make the conversation flow naturally, and don't let the prospect on the other end even guess that your next sentence is sitting in front of you.

Now despite all the talk about keeping it casual, there are still some specifics that apply to anyone in sales.

Here we've scaled them down, because your goal on the phone is not to sign someone up for a listing or persuade them to buy a particular house. All you're trying to do is make them willing to meet with you. Remember your goal: *You're not selling a listing; you're selling an appointment.*

Elements of a Good Script

You do need to plan. And when you sit down with a pencil and paper, these are the areas you have to cover:

The Opening

Most of the next chapter is devoted to how to handle the opening. Right now, think of your opening as setting the stage for the rest of the call. Beginning with a friendly and casual greeting, you let the prospect know right away who you are and what company you represent.

The Attention-Getting Remark or Reason for Calling

If you're not feeling too sharp, you may want to try to launch the conversation with a nebulous remark like, "I understand you just moved into your home. Could I ask you a few questions?"

At times, all of us fall back on the market research approach. But doing it can be misleading; because in a minute or so, you're going to tell that person why you're really calling. And they're going to feel you wasted their time.

Personally, I prefer having something a little more substantial to offer and making that known right off the bat.

The Benefits of Listening

In this section, the persuasion really begins. Now you have not only a proposal, but you also have the reasons necessary to back it up.

Couching everything from the point of view of the person you're talking to, you stick to the reasons why what you're offering can help them.

Essentially, you're turning their attention into interest because you're suggesting something that will benefit them personally.

But keep it short and sweet. Some experts say you shouldn't mention more than two or three advantages. Otherwise, they might find it confusing.

The Questions

At this point you begin to build up the prospect's trust in you by showing how interested you are in him or her. Asking specific questions, keying into their responses, picking up on the tone or inflection in their voices — you're making them like you.

But there's another advantage, too. Often within a few minutes, you'll be able to dig up what the motivating force is in their personality, at least as far as real estate is concerned. It may be money or security or status or comfort. Without even knowing it, they'll be telling you the points you need to emphasize.

The Objections

Most often, objections are the real estate agent's biggest headache — until they realize that everyone has objections to everything. Some sales pros recommend seeing an objection as a sign of interest. Maybe that's true.

Whether it is or not, you have an obligation to try to pierce through their negativity and show them the positive side of what you're offering.

A word of caution: If you run into someone who doesn't have any objections, put up your guard. Chances are they'll run out on you before the sale closes. They just didn't have the courage to tell you their true feelings face-to-face.

The Critical Close

In farming by phone, the close is your attempt to set up an appointment.

You may bring it up 30 seconds into the call. You may wait until two minutes into the call. When you decide to start to close is up to you.

If you wait for the prospect to do it, you'll be on the line forever.

Now don't be discouraged if the prospect doesn't seem to hear you at first. Hardly anyone ever closes the first time around.

You need to be patient — and persistent.

The Wrap-Up

As unlikely as it seems, the last 15 seconds of a call can be as critical as the first 15 seconds.

This is where you tread familiar ground once again, as you confirm the date and time of the appointment, mention anything you promised to bring along, make sure they have your name and number, and thank the prospect for their time.

Under less fortunate circumstances, you may be limited to reciting their major objection once again, repeating the great benefits of what you're offering, and thanking them for their time. Here you may also want to mention that you'll be getting in touch with them again in a few months, just to see if anything has changed.

If you look back over this structure, you'll see that a good farming call tries to do four things. Deviate from this order and you're in trouble. They are:

- Get attention
- Stimulate interest
- Arouse desire
- Go for the appointment

When thinking about your script, don't think of it as a sales presentation. If it's going to work, you have to think of it as a persuasive interview. It is an interview because there has to be give and take. If you wind up doing all the talking, you might as well close down shop.

You're not in the business of making *yourself* feel good. Your real aim has to be to make other people feel good. When you do, you'll find that you feel better, too.

How to Use a Script

Now we're getting very practical. What kind of paper should we use for our scripts? And how can we organize it so we can find what we need in a hurry?

Remember, a good script is only about three minutes long. But at the same time, you need to have all of your alternatives at your fingertips.

Some people prefer to write out their scripts on long pieces of paper, stapling them together and putting them into binders or on flip charts.

That's okay for the word-to-word types, but not for us. Real estate salespeople need more flexibility.

The answer? Once again, the popular index card. The backbone of our farm file, the cards now turn into the most convenient and easiest way to keep our scripts.

However, I'd recommend using the 3-by-5 cards for the scripts, instead of the 4-by-6 versions we suggested for your files. On each card, you're only going to have a sentence or two. And you won't be taking all those notes you need for your other files.

Index cards are ideal, because you can color-code them to each section of the script. For example, your breakdown might look like this:

Script Section:	*Color Code:*
Opening	Blue
Attention-Getting Remark, or Reason for Calling	Orange
Benefits	Pink
Objections	Yellow
Close	Green
Wrap-Up	White

Once you've finished divvying up your script sections and filling out the cards, you'll probably want to slip them into plastic covers or sleeves, and keep them in an indexed three-ring binder or on a large Rolodex.

That way you can flip quickly to the section you need next. Remember, during a phone call, you don't have a lot of time. Another advantage of the cards is that they're easy to revise and update. Just take out the one you don't like and slip in the new one.

Personally, I like to keep the old ones tucked away in my files. Every so often, I take them out to see how my approach has changed over time. It's a good way to learn.

If you're a computer buff, it's probably best to save

those skills for your farm directory. Usually the only phone scripts kept on computers are word-for-word and logical flow types.

Using the computer just makes changes more cumbersome.

Sample Scripts

Now let's get into some sample scripts. Of the two that follow, each is slightly different. It's good that our call outlines are only that — outlines to give us a solid start and direction. For the rest of it, it's up to you to use your instincts and experience to channel the conversation the way you want it to go.

Don't get stuck on the outline of script elements in the preceding sections. Use it as a guide, not a command.

Script 1

It's 9:30 a.m. Realtor Andrea Wilson came in early today, getting set up for her session of farming by phone. Ready on her desk are her neatly completed farm files, a Multiple Listing Book, charts on the latest mortgage rates, pens, pencils, notepaper, and her address book. The office is still quiet.

Her first call is to Patricia Evans, who lives in a 2,000-square-foot brick home. The bicycles and toys in the front yard indicate there are several children in the family. The home is well kept and fairly expensive.

The Opening

Agent: Good morning, is Patricia Evans at home?

Prospect: This is Patricia Evans.

Identifying Self and Company

Agent: Mrs. Evans, my name is Andrea Wilson, and I'm with Sell & Save Realty here in town. Do you have a minute to talk?

Prospect: No longer than that.

The Attention-Getting Remark

Agent: Mrs. Evans, I was hoping that you could do me a favor.

Prospect: What is it?

The Reason for Calling

Agent: Last Monday, Paul and Veronica Townsend came into my office. You may know them. They live in that wonderful English Tudor home on Spring Street — the one with the brick sidewalks and box hedges. Anyway, the Townsends are moving back to Boston. And they've asked me to help them find a new owner for their home.

If you've ever been in it, you know how comfortable the home is. With four bedrooms, everyone in the family has their own room, and it has lovely French doors opening onto an enormous patio.

And, because the Townsends have to be in Boston early next month, they're eager to find someone. So they're offering to help finance it. Do you happen to know any families who might be interested?

Prospect: There's a possibility. How much is it?

Overcoming Objection 1

Agent: If you consider using the equity in someone's present home (which could be quite substantial, given the rapid appreciation of homes in this area), and the Townsends' willingness to help with the financing, the monthly payments could be surprisingly low — I would guess around $1,500 a month. And that's what a lot of people in your neighborhood are paying for much smaller homes.

Prospect: It sounds interesting. Let me think it over and I'll get back to you.

Overcoming Objection 2 (or the Trial Close)

Agent: Mrs. Evans, I'd be happy to take you through the home. When you see it, perhaps you'll think of someone right away who would love it. It's as beautiful on the inside as it is on the outside. Would tomorrow be a good day or would you prefer Wednesday?

Prospect: Well, I guess it couldn't hurt. Why don't we make it Wednesday about 2 p.m.?

The Wrap-Up

Agent: That's perfect, Mrs. Evans. You live at 29442 Circle Drive, don't you?

Prospect: Yes, the gray house with white shutters.

Agent: Fine, I'll be there Wednesday at 2 p.m. Now my name is Andrea Wilson, and if you need to reach me before Wednesday, my phone number is 882-2405. Mrs. Evans, I want to thank you for your time and I look forward to seeing you.

Prospect: Thank-you. Good-bye.

Prospect: CLICK.

Agent: CLICK (Andrea hangs up last).

Script 2

Peter Lincoln decides to build this week's farming by phone session around the new low mortgage rates. His goal is to help people see that they could be getting more house for the same amount of money they're paying now. Working to his advantage is the fact that he knows the year everyone bought their homes and the approximate rates at those times. At 6:30 p.m., he starts calling.

The Opening

Agent: Hello, is Mr. Bellflower home?

Child: Just a minute — Dad, it's for you.

Prospect: Hello?

Identifying Self and Company

Agent: Good evening, Mr. Bellflower. My name is Peter Lincoln, and I'm with Citizen Realty here in Munster. Do you have a moment to speak on the phone?

Prospect: What's this about?

The Attention-Getting Remark

Agent: Mr. Bellflower, it's about you.

Prospect: What about me?

Agent: As you may be aware, in the past few weeks, home mortgage rates have been dropping dramatically. In fact, just today they hit 8 1/2%. You bought your home in 1981, didn't you? When rates were about 13%?

Prospect: I'm paying 12 1/2%.

Questions

Agent: Mr. Bellflower, have you considered that you and your family could be living in a larger, more spacious home for the same monthly payments you're making now?

If you've ever wanted a pool, another bedroom, maybe a study or a den, it's a great time to do it. Mr. Bellflower, may I ask how many children you have?

Prospect: Three and another on the way.

Agent: Well, congratulations. How old are your children?

Prospect: My two boys are four and six, and I have daughter who's eight.

More Probing Questions

Agent: With a growing family, a little more room couldn't hurt, could it? Tell me, what do you look for in a home?

Prospect: Personally, I like a yard that's easy to care for and a big garage so I can work in it.

Agent: Your work in the garage, is it woodwork or something else?

Prospect: Mostly cabinetwork. I'm a frustrated cabinetmaker. The only one who'll use what I make is my wife.

Agent: Well, Mr. Bellflower, if you'd like a home with plenty of room for your workshop and your children, there are two or three right in your neighborhood that might interest you.

Trial Close

Prospect: Would you like to have a look at them over at my office Saturday afternoon, or would Thursday evening at your home be more convenient?

Prospect: I have to talk to my wife about this.

Overcoming the Objection (Second Trial Close)

Agent: I understand, Mr. Bellflower. Buying a home is an important decision and the two of you need to make it together.

However, wouldn't it help to see the facts and figures? In just a few minutes, you can see for yourself how much more house you can get for your money in today's market. Now which is better for you, Thursday or Saturday?

Prospect: I guess, Saturday.

Agent: Saturday it is. Is 1 p.m. okay?

Prospect: That's fine.

The Wrap-Up

Agent: All right. Saturday at 1 p.m. It's Peter Lincoln and my office is at 3808 Turtle Rock Drive. Do you know how to get here?

Prospect: That's next to the Osco Drugs, isn't it?

Agent: That's the place. If you need to reach me before then, my number here is 648-2351.

Mr. Bellflower, I want to thank you for your time. And I'm looking forward to meeting you and your wife.

Prospect: Good-bye.

Prospect: CLICK.

Agent: CLICK (Peter hangs up last).

Practice, Practice

You can't escape it, no matter how hard you try. If you want to come across as smooth, relaxed, and polished, you have to practice.

Think of yourself as a pianist. Behind every flawless performance there are hours and hours of pounding away at the keyboard.

You won't have to put in as much time as performers do. But you will have to give it that wholeheartedness which separates the mediocre from the great.

Essential for your practice is a tape cassette recorder — just the standard $30 version will do. We're not aiming here at the quality of the sound. All we want is for you to hear back what you plan to say to your farm on the phone.

Once you've written your script, slap in a cassette, and push the "record" button.

Just read it to yourself the way you would speak it. When you've finished, play it back.

First listen to the sound and quality of your voice. Is it pleasing to you? Can you spot things you'd like to improve? Ask someone else's opinion, too.

After you've critiqued the sound, think about the content. Does the script seem to flow naturally? Are there places where it's rough, or where it sounds a little staged?

Work those out and then get a partner to role-play with you. Have several scripts ready, so you can pick out which elements are strongest.

It's a good idea also to draw up a list of the most common objections you expect to hear.

With the help of your partner, act out several scripts with you in the role of the agent. Then switch over to play the prospect. Just say what you would say if someone was calling your home.

After a few times, you'll be able to spot the weaknesses in your script and fix them. It also is wise to ask the advice of a few other people — maybe other agents in your office.

Remember, not everyone sees the world the way you do. They may hit on another response that'll crop up more frequently than you expect.

As you're practicing and evaluating the cassettes, try to think of yourself as walking a fine line.

You have to be assertive, but not aggressive. Knowledgeable but not conceited. Warm but still professional.

Through the warmth of your voice, the softness of your words, and the colorfulness of your speech, you can take control and lead the way without being perceived as pushy or obnoxious.

It's not just what you say, it's how you say it. Work as hard on that as you do on the script itself.

By the time you finish, you should've developed an almost instinctive response to any objection or question you may meet.

Your goal is: No matter where the prospect pulls away from the conversation, you should be able to gently and persuasively get them back on track. Guiding them along with you, you keep heading for the close. After a time, you'll become so good at it you won't even realize what you're doing. And neither will your prospect.

Don't Be Afraid to Change

Once we've poured a few hours of work into something, it can be hard to change it. But in this business, look for what works best. If you don't hit it the first time, keep trying.

Don't think your words are etched in eternity. Writing a script is personal, but it's also supposed to be profitable. Don't let your pride stand in the way of your performance.

If your scripts are not working as well as you'd like, you might want to ask someone else in your office to help you evaluate them.

If you're not satisfied with a script, think about doing some of the things that follow:

Simplify Your Offer

Sometimes we get caught up in our words, knowing full well what they mean, but forgetting that to others they may not be as clear.

For example, suppose you're asking:

"Mrs. Page, you've owned your home for six years. Would you be interested in a free home market evaluation?"

Now she's wondering:

"What on earth is he talking about?"

But she says:

"I don't think so. Good-bye."

Consider this approach:

"Mrs. Page, you've been in your home for six years. Wouldn't you like to know how much your home is worth today?"

Then sail straight into the benefits of knowing the home's value in the current market.

Add a Sense of Urgency

Sometimes we overlook the need to press people into action. You can recite all the advantages in the world, but if you don't give a reason to act now, forget it.

Your failure to create a sense of urgency can easily slip by unnoticed — until you start tallying your results!

For example, in the sample script with Peter Lincoln and Mr. Bellflower, we could've added this thought:

"You know, Mr. Bellflower, experts are

saying that the rates are only going to stay this low a few months. If you'd like a larger home, for the same amount of money, it's important to start looking as soon as possible."

Strengthen the Close

As you'll see later, there are all kinds of ways to close a call. Just an extra word or two, and you can make your close stronger.

Instead of:

"Which would be more convenient for you, Wednesday or Thursday?"

Try:

"I'd love to show you what's new on the market. I can be at your home Thursday evening. Is seven o'clock all right or is eight better?"

Soften the Lead-In

There's a chance you might be coming on too strong, sounding too pushy. If you think that's a problem, try softening the way you start.

If you're leading off with a matter-of-fact statement about benefits, switch to something along these lines:

"Mr. Keil, have you ever thought about how you could use the equity you've built up in your home to make money for you?"

Pause a brief moment and then coast right on into what you want to say.

Change the Offer

Of course, this is one change you'll probably be reluctant to make, because it involves the most work. But if your friends or family tell you the offer is weak, think of a new one.

If the offer focuses on size, switch to finances. If it's security, go for special features. If it's convenience, try prestige.

There are hundreds and hundreds of offers you can make. Be original. Take the time to stand out from the crowd.

Summary

Now we've begun to zero in on the specifics of how you can improve your farming by phone.

First, we discussed the importance of writing a script, not a word-by-word script, more like play-by-play — a general guideline to keep you on the right track.

Why should you use a script? Because a script:

1. Gives you a plan of action
2. Helps you overcome objections
3. Makes your presentation consistent
4. Helps you organize your thoughts logically
5. Helps you keep the client's perspective in mind
6. Produces better results

Every script needs certain elements. They are:

1. An opening
2. Attention-getting remark or reason for calling
3. Benefits of listening
4. Questions
5. Ways to overcome objections
6. A Close
7. A Wrap-up

Keeping the elements of your scripts on index cards gives you the flexibility you need to quickly find the right words at the right time.

9. The Opening

Getting started on the right foot is important, especially if you're not interested in having any receivers banged down in your ear.

We all know what a difference first impressions can make. On the phone, you have 15 seconds — *one fourth of a minute!* — to make it or break it.

In that brief time, you're obliged to capture the prospect's attention, identify yourself and your firm, give the reason for your call, and prevent your prospect from hanging up on you.

The Critical First 15 Seconds

Some clever salespeople try to weasel their way into a call by avoiding saying who they are and why they dialed that number.

Few things in life are more frustrating than having someone you're not really interested in talking to, keep you on the line with a bunch of questions you don't really want to answer.

Today telemarketing experts all agree: Tell the prospect who you are right off the top. Don't try to lure him or her into talking to you; it simply won't work. If you fool somebody in the first 15 seconds, are they ever going to believe you again?

Use Your Prospect's Name

The first words out of your mouth, of course, should be the prospect's name.

If you're positive a child has answered the phone, ask for Mr. Ralph or Mrs. Ralph. Pick one or the other, don't let the child do it for you.

More often than not, you won't be sure who's answering. Then a good way to start is by asking, "Mr. Ralph?" ending on an uplifted note.

If it is Mr. Ralph, he'll say, "Speaking."

If it's not, the person will either go find him or tell you he's not in. In that case, you may ask to speak to Mrs. Ralph.

Using the prospect's name as a question makes you sound more upbeat and enthusiastic. You're thought of as optimistic and eager to talk, which is a compliment to the listener.

If the prospect's name is hard to pronounce, fumble your way through it. Chances are that he or she will correct you and when they do, write it down phonetically so you can keep referring to it throughout the call.

Introduce Yourself and Your Firm

As soon as you've established you're talking to the right person, it's time to introduce yourself. Usually the best way is to give your name, then the name of your company.

If your company has a strong advertising campaign or it's known for a particular quality, you may want to toss in another phrase to better identify whom you work for. But avoid any trite sayings like, "This is Joe Jones with Smith Realty, the sell-more-homes people."

I would introduce the company first only under one condition — if your name is unusual or hard to pronounce. In this case, you might also want to add a little phrase to help someone remember it.

For example, you might say, "I'm with Dickinson Realty and my name is Jeffrey Christmas — just like the holiday."

The trick here is to keep it short.

Your greetings are friendly, warm, and casual, without a hint that you're trying to sell something.

In addition, your tone should be purposeful and direct, but not aggressive. Right from the start, you set the tone by what you say and how you say it.

Ask for a Moment of Your Prospect's Time

With the formalities out of the way, you repeat the prospect's name again, and then politely tell him or her how long you expect the call will take.

Here are some introductory phrases that come in handy:

"Mr. Michels, do you have a few minutes to talk?"

"Mrs. Williams, is this a convenient time to talk for a minute or two?"

"Mr. Smith, could you give me a few moments of your time?"

Almost everyone will say yes. If they don't, ask for a time when you can call back. They'll probably ask what you want to talk about and, in a second, you'll be into your script.

At this point, some overeager salespeople like to prolong the pleasantries with "How are you today?" While some people will disagree with me, I think this is a fatal error. If a perfect stranger is calling me, I know they don't really care how I am and I don't really want to tell them. All I want to know is why they dialed my number and asked for me.

Of course, if you've been farming this turf for awhile and personally know the prospects, then some pleasantries would certainly would be appropriate.

Boiling it down to the basics, the first few seconds of each call should go like this:

- Use your prospect's name
- Give your name
- Identify your company
- Repeat your prospect's name
- Ask for a moment of their time

What to Say Next

Now comes the critical moment when you start laying yourself on the line. If what you say makes the prospect think you want to sell him something that's going to cost him money, forget it. No matter how good the house or property is, without persuasion you haven't got a prayer.

But if you lead the prospect to believe that you want to talk about something important to him or her — like a vital problem they have that you can help them with — they're likely to pay attention.

There are a number of ways to start off the

147

conversation. Here you're trying to do one of two things: (1) convince him or her of the benefits of listening or (2) establish rapport.

The approach you choose depends partly on your personality and partly on the specific characteristics of your farm. If it's a chummy sort of place, where people like to get to know each other, building rapport isn't bad.

But if it's an area of estates and high-priced homes, go for the benefits-of-listening approach.

To give you an idea of how to get into it, here are a few suggestions.

The Benefits-of-Listening Approach

Using this approach takes you directly into the heart of what you're trying to do. Lead off with the strongest benefit you have in your arsenal. You might want to begin with something like this:

> *"I'd like to talk to you about reducing your monthly mortgage payment."*

> *"If you'd like to start having your money work for you, instead of your landlord, . . ."*

> *"I'm calling to tell you about something that could give you and your family financial security."*

For a softer approach, try a thought-provoking question, such as:

> *"Have you ever wondered what you would do if . . . ?"*

"Have you ever stopped to think about . . . ?"

"Do you want your family . . . ?"

If you choose to plunge right into the benefits of how you can help them, be sure to cushion your words so they make the prospects feel that there's something they can do to change their own lives and make them better.

Give people a sense of power over their future. Offer them an opportunity to take decisive, beneficial action. Help them see the difference it can make in their lives, and you'll see a difference in your life, too.

Some agents prefer a two-step approach to farming by phone. They start off with a remark aimed at building up rapport with the prospect. The approach you choose depends in part on how you think the individual prospect will respond. Choose the approach that will allow him or her to respond most favorably.

The Rapport-Building Approach

Here are some hints for a rapport-building opening.

Refer to Your Mailing — Many real estate agents send a regular newsletter or other mailing to their farms. If you do a regular mailing, it's a point of contact you can refer to in the first few moments of the call.

For example, if last month's newsletter had a big spread on home improvements in the neighborhood, mention it. Then lead into an offer related to it — perhaps, as we suggested earlier, a free market evaluation based on some remodeling you spotted while driving by.

But be sure that you mention the newsletter for a reason. Don't just use it as an excuse to make you more credible. Remember, your prospects don't care about your credibility. They want to know what you can do for them.

Refer to an Ad Campaign —If you're handling a new development, condominium complex, or vacation time-sharing concept that has received extensive media attention, mention it.

Maybe there's a catchy phrase or good-looking footage that will bring the project into the prospect's mind.

But be sure to follow up quickly with something more substantial. Don't let it be, "Have you ever considered owning a second home?"

Instead, try something like, "Did you know that despite the recent tax revision, there are still considerable tax benefits to owning a second home?"

Mention a Referral — Nothing opens more doors for you than using someone's name as a referral. There's no better way to start off a call than, "You know Andrew Thompkins, don't you? He suggested that I give you a call."

Immediately you have created a link between you and the caller — a mutual friend or acquaintance.

Announce a New Listing — All of us are basically curious about our neighbors and neighborhoods. If you have a new listing, call the neighbors nearby and let them know you're handling the listing. It's a courtesy, but it's also a great way for you to find out names of prospective buyers.

If you miss the opportunity to call the neighbors before the "for sale" sign goes up, call and invite them to the open house.

Make a Personal Reference — If you know anything at all about the person you're calling or the location where they live, try to use it at the beginning of the call.

The more genuine and complimentary you are, the better they'll like it. Something like this is sure to ease the path: "I read in the local paper the other day that you recently got a promotion — congratulations!"

Once again, you're showing a degree of personal interest that sets you apart from other real estate agents. And, at the same time, you're appealing to their ego.

Refer to a Recent Neighborhood Event — You would use an opening like this with a special offer — for example, the Home-Protection Kit we mentioned a few chapters back. You might offer this kit after a crime in the neighborhood, or after a fire or other emergency.

Starting off this way makes you seem a part of the neighborhood. And that's how you want people to think of you.

Dramatic events, however, must be handled carefully as you don't want people to think you're capitalizing on someone else's misfortune. Life insurance salespeople garnered a bad reputation for passing out business cards at funerals.

Ask a Favor — A good way to build rapport is to ask a favor of your prospect — for example, "I wonder if you could do me a favor." Hardly anyone will turn you down. And right from the beginning of the call, you're enlisting them on your side. It's personal and warm, but it only works if you hold onto that note through the rest of the call; so be especially careful with the line that follows.

Don't start off enlisting the prospect's help and

then immediately turn it into a hard sales pitch. If you do, you'll leave a very sour impression.

In a farm situation, especially one which has had some time to develop, asking a favor can be a very effective opening.

Sparking Their Interest

Once you've captured their attention, it's time to start developing that attention into interest. Interest develops when you begin to show someone how you can help them personally.

Remember, as soon as you identify yourself on a call, your prospect is wondering what this real estate agent can do for him or her.

Related to that question are some others: Why should I be listening? What is this all about? Who else has this person helped? Is this legitimate? Is this person sincere?

Most often, you're not going to be greeted with a warm and friendly "hello." Usually it will be polite, but with an air of suspicion.

Subconsciously, many of us think that other people are out to get whatever they can from us. Unfortunately, often experience has proved that to be true.

But it's *not* hard to dispel their suspicions. Not if you use the right tone of voice and say the right words. In a few seconds, that psychological distance can turn into warmth, once they see that your primary focus is to help them.

Remember, you can use many methods to spark a prospect's interest, but always focus your words on what you can do for the prospect.

Emphasize the Greatest Benefits

As a real estate professional, it's your job to point out to people what you perceive to be the biggest advantages to them. In any real estate decision, there are probably as many advantages to acting as there are reasons for staying put — and, of course, it's easier for people to stay put.

Often what many agents play up first are the financial aspects of home ownership — such as lowering monthly mortgage payments, moving to nicer home, or the possible appreciation in the prospect's current residence.

But don't limit yourself to financing alone. Just as some people like jazz music and others like rock and roll, different offers will appeal to different prospects. See which one appeals most to the people you serve.

Once you find a winner, stick with it. That's not always as easy as it sounds, because you're going to get tired of the offer long before your prospects do. Telling the same offer to a 300-home farm gets quite repetitive; but remember, it's the first time for the prospect.

At the same time, don't be surprised if what works perfectly one day all of a sudden stops working. People change and so, too, does the market. So be ready to try out new appeals.

One final note: While you generally want to use your biggest benefit at the beginning of the call, it's often best to save your second biggest benefit for the end of the call — especially if you generated interest from your first benefit.

By saving a benefit for the end of a call you can help whet the appetite for an in-person visit. But use whatever approach works best for you.

Keep Your Opening Short and Direct

In addition to appealing to personal needs, your opening remarks need to be short and to the point. Why? Because people lose interest — fast.

And the minute they lose interest and their minds start to wander, you've lost them. So keeping right on target, leading the prospect through a logical sequence will help keep them with you.

Stress How You Can Help Them

As the friendly persuader, you not only want to encourage people to act, you also want them to ask you to help them.

But you don't want to play up yourself too much. So you build in little motivators, things like using the word "we." Or you toss in a phrase about how "I helped your neighbors down the street." Or "You know, the Jones got wonderful financing."

Use words and ideas that build you up without making you sound boastful.

The best way to achieve this is to assume from the beginning that your prospect is going to use your services. So you couch all your language to that end. It's simple and subtle and it works.

Get a Dialog Going

Over and over again, we've said that you can't use the word "you" too often.

When you're dealing with real estate, especially with homes, you're involved with something very personal. It's not like calling a factory and offering a new kind of drill bit for one of their machines.

It's something that is going to make a big difference in the quality of a person's life — something they want so badly they're usually willing to invest their entire savings in it. This isn't your decision. It's your prospect's decision. But you can help by showing him or her that there is a decision to be made and what some of their options are. You lead the way, but never push people down the path.

Explain the Advantages of Owning a Home

When marshaling your persuasive skills, first think about why anyone should want to own a home. Here are some very practical reasons.

Protection Against Inflation

How many times have you heard stories starting off with "If only I had bought that house way back when?"

Real estate is one investment that has, over the years, kept pace or in many areas even exceeded the inflation rate.

Just the other day, I heard about lots which sold for $5,000 when the land was just being developed. Today, about 10 years later, the average lot price is $150,000. Quite a dramatic return, isn't it?

While homes aren't generally sold as true investments, one of the logical precepts for owning a home (versus renting) is that the home will appreciate in value.

Tax Benefits

With Congress closing most of the loopholes with the latest tax reform, buying a home is one of the few investments left that spares you from giving it to the government.

There's something very American about owning your own home — something that's part of the American dream. It's so precious to us, not even Congress would touch it.

This line of persuasion is especially effective when dealing with renters, many of whom would be surprised if you sat down with a pencil and paper and had them figure out how much their tax savings from the mortgage interest deduction would be.

In addition, as people move up to larger homes — with larger mortgages — their interest deduction also increases.

Low Initial Investment

While most lenders prefer 20% down, many times a buyer can purchase a home for as little as 10% (or even 5%) down. And even that number can be decreased with seller financing.

Putting $9,000 down (10% of a $90,000 house) or $850 a month sounds a lot -more palatable than talking about a selling price of nearly $100,000.

Huge Potential Market

The other day, I was reading about Century 21's efforts to penetrate the housing market in Japan.

One of their biggest problems is the fact that in the Japanese culture, families tend to hang on to their homesteads for centuries. Therefore, there aren't many houses available to sell.

Fortunately, we don't have to deal with that problem. Houses change hands in this country almost as quickly as cars do. And the idea of handing down a title deed to our children and grandchildren is usually one of the furthest things from our minds.

By contrast, most people are more interested in getting the equity out of their homes than in making it a heritage. So anyone who buys a home knows that there will always be someone looking for a home.

In other words, we don't have to worry that the demand will dry up.

Personal Independence

Having your own home is a mark of independence. You can decorate it as you will, add on, take away, put in a garden, do whatever you like and, as long as you don't violate city statutes, no one can do a thing about it.

A long time ago, I was renting a small stucco home, with interesting accents that I thought added to its character. One of those was an ancient kitchen with enormous solid wood cabinets and a wonderful tile sink.

When I moved in, the landlady made it sound as though she would own the property the rest of her days. Four years later, she sold it to someone who preached the virtues of older homes, but did everything in his power to modernize them as cheaply as he could.

He thought my lovely, character-filled kitchen was an atrocity. One day, he informed me he was going to modernize it. One month later, the cheapest butcher block cabinets you can buy were installed, together with fluorescent lighting.

When I walked in after a few weeks away, I decided on the spot that I had to own my own home.

Many, many other people have similar stories.

Forced Savings

All of us need housing and all of us need to save money for the future. The best way to meet those two needs is through home ownership.

When someone pays rent, it's the same as putting it in the landlord's pocket. But when you own a home, you're putting some money (exclusive of the interest on the mortgage loan) into your own pocket.

Down the road, you can sell the home and most likely get that money back. If you're over 55, you don't even have to pay taxes on your first $100,000 profit. It's a painless and easy way to prepare for your retirement.

Flexibility

Often a big objection to owning a home is the lack of flexibility. People think of ownership as tying them down. But that's not realistic.

As a homeowner, you can always choose to rent out your home. Sometimes such rentals even generate a positive cash flow.

If you don't want the hassle of managing your home as a rental property, there are plenty of people you can hire to do that.

Remember, people in this country usually move once every four to five years. So a house isn't the albatross that some people think it is.

Trade-In Value

When we trade in our cars, usually we trade up to a bigger and better model. The same thing is true with houses. Of course, here the tax law encourages us to do so.

People can think of their houses as stepping stones on their way up to the home of their dreams. By trading in their homes every few years as their income rises, someday they can have everything they've ever wanted in a home.

It's a lot easier to do it this way than to save your pennies, hoping that eventually you'll have that huge down payment.

Describe the Unique Features of a Home

Now that we've refreshed your memory as to the advantages of owning a home, let's move on to why people pick the homes they do.

One reason stands out: People are always looking for a larger home.

It's the "law of rising expectations." We always want something a little bigger or better than what we have now. Nations, as well as families, are motivated by that principle.

In looking for a home, the first thing people notice is, of course, the price. Generally, they have a fixed idea of what they feel they can afford to pay.

But when a home wins their hearts, it's because of its unique features — special features that buyers look for and are willing to pay more for.

These features include, but are of course not limited to, the following:

- Location
- Brick patios
- Landscaping
- Skylights
- Tile or shake roofs
- Hardwood floors
- Fireplaces
- Large closets
- Swimming pools
- Picture windows
- Modern baths
- Modern eat-in kitchens
- Laundry rooms
- Views

When a prospective buyer is walking through a home, features like these conjure up dreams of what life there would be like for their family. If you've ever seen a stone house built in the shape of a castle, would you guess the owner has fantasies of kingship?

Or maybe a pool is a symbol of their commitment to get themselves in shape. Or an eat-in kitchen may be a mark of family togetherness.

People buy a home because their hearts tell them to. And the things that move their hearts are love, security, recreation, economy, privacy, warmth, convenience, investment, and the very human desire to own.

If someone falls in love with a house, they'll hang in there through all the problems that can arise during a closing.

What's odd is that everybody falls in love with different houses, and one of your biggest jobs is figuring out how to make that magical moment happen for each and every one of your clients.

The Value of Referrals

While listings are the bread and butter of a real estate professional, referrals are the steak and potatoes. Referrals can give you more productive leads than anything else. And leads are critical to continued success in this business. That's one of the beauties of farming, too. Many of the neighbors know each other. They talk to each other frequently, and if one has found an agent he or she likes, others will follow the recommendation. Never minimize the importance of referrals in sales, and never forget to ask for them.

In fact, every time you talk to someone who is not currently in the market to buy or sell a home, ask if they have a friend, relative, or neighbor who is.

Essentially, referrals can work for you in two ways. Referrals can:

1. Get you good names for new prospects.
2. Strengthen your presentation by creating rapport from the beginning of the call, by adding specific examples to make you more persuasive, and by building your credibility.

Referrals Get Good Names for New Prospects

If someone gives you a name, chances are that the referral is thinking about making a move in real estate. Maybe they said something at a party or at work. Maybe they just had a baby and need more room. Whatever the reason, the person making the referral thinks you can help them.

This line of thinking makes sense, and statistics also prove it. In most businesses, 80% of the sales are generated from 20% of the customers.

After a few years, often salespeople don't have to continue prospecting, because their clients keep sending more people to them.

But the good salespeople still set aside time for making calls. They know that prospecting helps keep their own skills sharp and helps them stay in tune with what's happening in today's marketplace.

Conventional wisdom says that every time you close a sale, you should get three referrals. Some real estate professionals ask their clients to call the referrals at the time a deal closes. Usually it's best to ask them to call their friends, but do it during a special call a week or so after the closing.

If a person is having a hard time thinking of any referrals, you may want to jar his or her memory by asking something like, "What clubs do you belong to?" "Is there anyone you know in your club who might be interested in a new home?"

If they're reluctant to make the preliminary call themselves, don't force them. Just ask if it's all right to use their name when you call.

And remember, once you have a name, don't put it aside as something to get to when you have the time. Make a point of calling within a day or so. Chances are that your client has been talking anyway about the home they're buying or selling, and you want to call while those memories are still fresh.

Also, don't overlook the possibility of referrals from someone who just stops by the office.

One real estate agent got caught in a client's messy divorce situation that involved listing the home. It turned out that the wife, who gave him the listing, didn't really have the authority to do so. Within a few hours, he'd lost it.

But she mentioned that her attorney might be interested in buying some income property. The next day, the agent had a substantial client in that area.

Remember, every person you talk to associates with a couple hundred or more people on a semi-regular basis. That can generate a lot of potential clients.

Referrals Strengthen Your Presentation

Using referrals strengthens your presentation by building rapport, by giving you specific examples to work with, and by increasing your credibility.

Building Rapport — Using a referral to begin a call is great. Right from the start, you have something in common — a mutual friend.

Some of the suspicion disappears, and warmth often takes its place. After all, their friends wouldn't be recommending someone who didn't want to help them, would they? In addition, you're no longer an unknown voice at the other end of the wire. You're someone who's got a recommendation behind you.

Remember the old adage: It's not *what* you know but *who* you know that gets you places.

In addition to all of the above, having someone refer you to one of their friends means that they valued your service. That will make you feel good. And that good feeling will come through in the extra self-confidence that radiates from your voice during your call.

Giving You Specific Examples to Use — You can also use referrals indirectly by pointing out specific examples of whatever you're discussing during a call.

If you mention someone the referral knows or who lives down the street, your point carries a lot more weight. Remember the line, "I recently had the pleasure of helping the Joneses find a new home?"

If you get into a tight spot during the call, a way to handle it is by referring to someone else's situation. For example, they might say, "We just can't afford it right now."

You might respond, "I understand why you feel that way. So did the Witherspoons, until they saw how easy it was to use the equity in their home and move into a home that was much roomier for their family. They said they never would have dreamed it possible to be living the way they are now."

Any debater knows that specifics always strengthen his or her argument. We all love to hear about the good things that happen to other people. Secretly, we think maybe those good things could happen to us, too.

Don't overlook the very basic human interest in other people's stories. Keep tabs on stories like that and use them. You may even want to jot down a few to slip into your script binder. They'll give your prospects hope.

Building Credibility — People in your farm can't go to the local library and look up a chart that shows which realtors are the biggest producers in town.

I don't think that would matter much anyway.

What they're looking for is a real estate agent who puts their interests first — the kind of agent who takes the time to give them personal, one-to-one attention. You can't put a yardstick to that kind of service and publish it in a book.

But you can make a very effective statement about it through word of mouth. Some salespeople ask clients to sign letters of referral. They prepare them, then whip them out when the sale is concluded, asking for a signature.

Letters like that can be useful during face-to-face

interviews. You can leave them for prospects to study and keep. It's a good idea to have five to ten letters of recommendation in your briefcase at all times.

When you're farming by phone, though, letters won't work.

However, a reasonable variation is to ask a prospect if he or she would, on occasion, be willing to talk to some of your other clients. If you do get someone to agree with you on this (and you should get a few), don't overuse it. Save it for those critical times when you have a prospect right on the leading edge of doing business with you.

The nature of our business involves building a relationship with a client; and, truthfully, we ask them to place a lot of trust in us.

If we're remiss in our efforts to sell their home or if we forget to check the computer printout of new listings every day specifically for them, we can cost a client thousands and thousands of dollars.

We invest in them and they invest in us. It's mutual.

Simply making an offer to put them in touch with previous clients implies that we can be trusted.

Of course, it's best to clear this with the other clients first. It doesn't hurt to ask people who are especially satisfied if they'd mind being used as a reference.

I wouldn't make it a practice of offering their names and numbers on all farming calls. But if you sense someone hovering on the brink of trusting you and you feel a good recommendation would make a difference, suggest it. It's best, of course, to suggest someone who is like your prospect or was in a similar situation.

Instead of 20 letters, have at hand 20 phone numbers of people you've cleared this with first.

I think you'll find that you won't give out the

numbers often, but when you do, they'll work wonders.

Don't forget to call the prospect back the next day and see if they contacted the client and would like to confirm an appointment.

Before we move on, say to yourself that at the close of every sale, you'll ask for three referrals. Get a head start on building up your farm the smart way.

Building Trust

Buying or selling real estate is complicated. It's not like someone signs a piece of paper, writes out a check, and that's it. It's a process. It can be long or short; but during the course of it, you build a relationship with your client. And that relationship begins with your first telephone call.

In addition to having the right facts, figures, and approach, you have to make your prospects trust you. And you have to do it the very first time they hear your voice.

Having trust in someone means you put your confidence in them. You're willing to rely on their information and judgement to help you make a decision.

With a child, trust is instinctive. With most adults, it's something you have to win.

In general terms, you win trust by showing that you understand them, that you know what you're talking about, and that you're genuinely interested in them. Sound familiar?

However, you have to be careful, because small missteps can destroy budding trust in an instant.

It can happen through dishonesty. If you're caught in even a very small white lie on that first call, there won't be any others.

If you say you're going to do something, then move heaven and earth to get it done. This is especially true if you promise to call someone back. They'll remember, even if you don't. And it'll rankle them that you didn't call.

If you have the good fortune to represent a well-known company, use it. But tread lightly here; you don't want to sound pompous.

Trust doesn't come by itself. You must earn it.

Summary

What you've just finished pointed the way to breaking the ice on those 15 first critical seconds of a call. As you saw, there are a number of ways to approach farming by phone.

But here are the rules for the first few seconds:

- Use the prospect's name
- Identify yourself and your company
- Repeat the prospect's name
- Be courteous and let them know how long the call will take

Now you have a choice. Will you hit them right off the top with the great benefits of your offer? Or will you opt for a softer-sell approach, trying instead to build up a sense of rapport and trust?

Either way can work well. Which approach you use depends on your own personality, the makeup of your farm, and the particular offer you're making.

Then we discussed some of the reasons why people buy homes and what they look for in particular homes. Remember, people don't buy because of what their head tells them to do; they follow their hearts. And when it comes to that, the special features of a home are what make the sale.

The secret of turning prospects into clients is to cultivate their trust in you. Although much of their confidence comes from things like what you say and how you say it, we gave you some practical tips on how to encourage it.

Best of all, you have a head start on building trust when the prospect you're calling is a referral.

In some businesses, 80% of the sales come from 20% of the customers, which shows you the value of referrals.

For the real estate professional, referrals can:

1. Expand your farm directory by adding new names for prospecting.
2. Strengthen your presentation by creating rapport at the beginning of the call, giving you specific examples that make you more persuasive, and helping establish your credibility.

Now that we've gotten you through the opening, let's see what comes next.

10. Questions Keep the Conversation Going

Once you begin a conversation, it's your responsibility to keep it going. Don't expect the prospect to start chatting merrily away.

To break down a prospect's initial resistance and create a warm and inviting atmosphere over the phone, nothing works better than questions.

Questions take some of the burden of talking off of you and put it on the prospect. You get to know each other, and that's what you need to figure out the best way to approach him or her about buying or selling a home.

How to Spot a Potential Seller or Buyer

In the first moments of a call, and after all the pleasantries are exchanged, you want to find out if the person you're talking to is a genuine prospect.

You can't tell just by asking, "Are you interested in selling your home?" or "Do you plan to buy a home anytime soon?"

Here the rule of thumb is simple: Virtually every

adult in this country uses, buys, or sells real estate. Therefore, your prospects are limitless. If someone isn't interested today, try them six months from now or a year from now. Keep working your farm until it pays the returns you want and deserve.

You can tell how good a prospect is at a particular time by asking questions — not the kind of questions we asked above. But the kind of question we ask to learn more about people.

All too often a salesperson finishes the greeting, makes his first remark, and shuts down shop when he hears the caller say, "I'm not interested."

If you believe that phrase every time you hear it, don't expect to be moving up in the real estate world. The prospect might be interested; he or she just might not know it yet.

Your response could be, "Have you ever considered that . . . ?" or a simple and direct, "Why not?"

Basically, all you want to do now is get the conversation going. Don't think to yourself, I've got to find out if this person is interested in buying or selling a home. Think instead, I'd like to get to know this person. Someday he or she could become a client.

If you've stated your reason for calling and the listener doesn't seem interested, keep them on the line with questions.

What Questions Can Do for You

Questions work wonders for a number of reasons. But most important, they help build a two-way conversation between you and your prospect.

Help You Stay Out of an Argument

If the prospect says something you don't agree with, don't let them know that. Instead find out why they feel that way. Behind every feeling, there's a reason. Ferreting out the reasons can tell us a lot about someone.

Give people credit for feeling the way they do. And respect them for it. In the long run, it'll help you in your work. You may very likely discover that people are a lot more sensitive and aware than you ever realized.

Remember, on farming calls, what matters most is how the prospect thinks and feels, not how you think and feel.

Keep You from Talking Too Much

By asking questions, you reduce the danger that you'll monopolize the conversation. That's something too many people in sales have yet to learn. Questions protect you from talking about yourself — and instead focus the attention on the other person.

It's an easy way to avoid a gigantic pitfall.

Let You Get to Know Each Other

When you're asking questions as a real estate professional, there are some basics you'll want to know. For example:

- Does the prospect own or rent his or her home?
- Is he or she single or married?
- How many people live in the home?

- How many children are there?
- How old are the children?
- What kind of work does the prospect do?
- How long has he or she lived in the home?
- Does the prospect tend to move every few years or so?
- What does he or she like about the neighborhood where he or she is now?
- What does the prospect like about this home?
- Does the prospect have financial resources outside of his or her employment?
- Would the prospect someday like to invest in real estate?

In your mind, questions like these help fill in the gaps in the prospect's portfolio. To know what kind of home people might be interested in, you have to know what kind of lifestyle they have and what they value.

People don't answer questions like that directly. You have to phrase them so they don't come across sounding threatening, but merely as "I'd like to get to know you better."

Once you have a handle on what interests a prospect, you'll know the best sales strategy to use. Although everyone is different, some things we all care about.

Help the Prospect Clarify His or Her Thinking

A good example of this is using questions to build a case for buying or selling a home for financial reasons. Many times people are not aware of new types of mortgages or of how a home can appreciate over time.

They need you to tell them. And the most

comfortable way is through questions. Then you avoid the unpleasant "But didn't you know that . . .?"

None of us like to feel stupid. Asking questions is a way to avoid that. It shows your concern for helping the prospect make the best decision.

Help People See What They Really Want

When I began looking for a home, I wanted a fixer-upper on a big lot, with room for a pool, lots of windows and at least one large tree. I wound up with a rebuilt house on a big lot where I can never put in a pool, almost a forest of trees, and skylights.

The lesson is: People seldom know what they really want — at least when it comes to buying a home. That's why building up a relationship is so important.

As you get to know someone, you'll develop a sense of what really matters to them and what doesn't.

Someone may think they don't want to sell their home, but if they could buy that big white Cape Cod down the street — and pay only $50 more a month — would they be interested then?

In every area of our lives, the world is full of options. It's our responsibility to make people aware of the real estate opportunities about to pass them by.

Make the Prospect Feel Important

Having interviewed hundreds of people, I know how flattering it is to have someone question you about yourself.

Very rarely does anyone come back with the response, "It's none of your business."

If they do, they're telling you something important

about themselves. Don't take it personally. It *is* your business, because you want to help make their lives better.

Think of how often you sit down with someone and they take the time to find out how you feel. For most of you, I bet it doesn't happen very frequently. All of us are so busy trying to hang on to our own wants, needs, and desires that we don't have time to bother about anyone else's.

If you take the time to find out how people feel, you'll find your work infinitely more rewarding.

People like to talk about themselves. They like to tell the story of how they found that special house and of all the trouble they went through to get it.

Listen when people talk to you, and you'll never be wondering what on earth to say next. The person who asks questions is the person who never stops learning.

It's trite but true that in real estate, the more you learn, the more you earn.

The Two Kinds of Questions

A long time ago, Socrates said that you sell more by asking people than by telling them. And basically there are two kinds of questions you can ask: (1) open-ended and (2) closed-ended.

Open-Ended Questions

In short, open-ended questions are questions that cannot be answered with either yes or no. They're probing questions which require the recipient to give more information.

They are used to keep the conversation flowing

and almost always start with words like these:

- Who
- What
- Where
- When
- Why
- Which
- How

As you can probably tell by the list, open-ended questions are the type reporters use in digging up a story.

By posing a question a certain way, you can start a prospect thinking. But the prospect will have the sense that he or she is thinking it out on his or her own.

People tend to pick up on the spirit in which you're asking them questions and they reflect it back to you. If you fill a question with interest and enthusiasm, you'll find the answer coming back the same way. If you ask a question matter-of-factly, expect a crisp and clear response.

In addition, when you ask questions, you have the opportunity to let a prospect know what you think. But you give them the satisfaction of showing that you care about what they think, too.

More often than not, you'll probably want to head into some open-ended questions soon after the beginning of a call. Unlike other people in sales, your primary focus is getting to know the people in your farm.

When you ask open-ended questions, don't be afraid to feed back a little information about yourself — not boastful information, but the kind that friends exchange when they're talking to each other.

If we open up, other people will open up to us.

You don't want to spill out your personal problems. That's a big no-no. But just as you're working to think of the prospect as an individual, with unique thoughts, dreams, and desires, the prospect wants to think of you as an individual, too.

Let your personality come across. Don't hide the real you. And you'll see others showing you their true colors, too.

Closed-Ended Questions

Closed-ended questions, on the other hand, are those which can be answered with yes or no. You employ these when you want more control in a conversation or need to get the prospect back on track.

Often in telemarketing, closed-ended questions are used in taking sales orders, confirming information, or setting up visits. They're highly structured and tend to sharply reduce rambling.

Closed-ended questions begin with words like:

- Is
- Do
- Has
- Can
- Are

Much more direct than open-ended questions, they let you steer the conversation directly where you want it to go.

Moreover, closed-ended questions have a few variations that can also be quite useful. They are the paraphrase and the tie-down.

The Paraphrase — The first variation is called the "paraphrase." When you ask this type of question, you echo back the prospect's own words. Here's an example:

Agent: In your income bracket, I'm surprised you haven't considered the possibility of investing in rental properties. May I ask why?

Prospect: Because of all the headaches that go into managing them.

Agent: Suppose you found a way to enjoy all the financial benefits of rental properties without the headaches that go into managing them. Then wouldn't you agree that rental properties are a sound investment for someone like yourself?

Similar to repeating a favorite word of the prospect's, paraphrasing their sentences fosters a sense of trust and caring, and helps the communication process. In a way, it's showing that you share a common outlook. It's subtle psychology that most people won't even know you're practicing. You see, people love their own words. And they think just the way they talk.

Paraphrasing is a great way to build on a client's remarks, but keep heading right towards your own objective: setting up an appointment.

The Tie-Down — Another way to set up a closed-ended question is by using what sales experts and trial attorneys call *tie-downs*. What you're tying down is the answer, because there's not much room for variation.

You can spot a tie-down when someone uses phrases like these:

- Aren't you?
- Don't you agree?
- Wouldn't it?
- Haven't you?
- Won't you?
- Isn't it?
- Can't you?

Tie-downs are a popular way of reducing sales resistance, and they work because they help people see things in a different light. But they aren't preachy. And the beauty of them is that if *you* say something, the prospect may doubt it. If the prospect says it, it's true.

In addition, tie-downs are a way of helping your prospects say the one word you want to hear — "yes."

When to Use Closed- and Open-Ended Questions

The best way to successfully farm by phone is to intertwine both closed and open-ended questions. Use the latter to build your relationships and warm the conversation. Use the former to keep the conversation on target and zero in on your close.

If you start off with closed-ended questions too early, you'll regret it; because if you give someone a chance to say no before you make your case, the odds are two to one that they will say no.

At the start, you want to use a number of open-ended questions to probe for small clues to the prospect's situation and outlook. Then you step up the pace of the call and zero in on the close with one or two tie-down, closed-ended questions.

Before moving on, a word of caution: Be gentle in

asking your questions. Your calls should not turn out to be interrogations, but should always be along the lines of friendly conversation.

To sharpen your skills at picking out closed- and open-ended questions, try your hand at this list.

1. Have you lived in this area long? (Closed (C))
2. Why did your family choose this neighborhood? (Open (O))
3. Don't you think this is a wonderful neighborhood for raising children? (C)
4. Do you ever take your children to the nearby city parks? (C)
5. How large is your home? (O)
6. Is it bigger than your previous house? (C)
7. What do you look for in a house? (O)
8. Are you originally from this area? (C)
9. If you could move anywhere in the city, where would it be? (O)
10. With interest rates dropping so quickly, wouldn't you agree that now is a good time to buy? (C)
11. What do you like best about your home now? (O)
12. What things would you change about it? (O)
13. Do you believe that real estate is a good investment? (C)
14. Have you considered the tax benefits of owning a second home? (C)
15. Why is it important for you to own your own home? (O)

To see how easy it is to switch from closed to open ended questions, take a look at the examples on the following page:

Closed: When you're looking for a home, are there any special features that are important to you?

Open: When you're looking for a home, what special features are most important to you?

Closed: Is it that your family must have three bedrooms?

Open: How critical is it that your family have three bedrooms?

Closed: Did you use a realtor to find your current home?

Open: How did you find your current home?

Closed: Do you like colonial-style homes?

Open: What style of home do you and your wife prefer?

On the other hand, there are times when you want to get the prospect back on track — to keep him or her from wandering too far from the subject of your open-ended questions. In this case, you'll switch from open- to closed-ended questions:

Open: When, during the week, is the best time for us to get together?

Closed: Would Thursday evening be a good time for us to meet? (Or would Saturday afternoon be better?)

Open: What kind of people do you think would be interested in an offer like that?

Closed: Do you know anyone who might be interested in such an offer?

Open: What did your last realtor not do for you?

Closed: Do you feel you got adequate service from your former realtor?

Open: What kinds of advantages do you see in renting?

Closed: Do you want to be renting nine months from now? Two years from now?

Learn to Listen

Listening well is an art — an art that I'm afraid many of us don't practice anymore. We're so preoccupied with our own thoughts, often we don't have time to listen to anyone else's.

If you want to succeed in real estate farming by phone, learning to listen should be at the top of your list.

But there's a trick to listening well: You have to have a sense of inner security strong enough to let the other person talk.

That sounds easier than it is. It's more than a matter of simply learning to keep our mouths shut. It also involves putting our egos to rest, at least for the duration of a call.

But if you improve the way you listen, you'll also improve your number of appointments.

What to Listen For

When you listen, you're looking for two things: (1) the content of what the person you're talking to is saying and (2) the feeling behind that content.

We reveal our feelings in the words we choose, the inflections in our voices, where we pause, and the sincerity behind what we're saying.

Inflections are a key to unlocking feelings. Take, for example, the sentences at the top of the next page:

I <u>don't want</u> to buy a new home.
I don't want <u>to buy</u> a new home.
I don't want to buy <u>a new home.</u>

Depending on where you place the inflection, the

meaning changes. If the emphasis is on "don't want," you need to probe for the real reason.

If "to buy" is underscored, maybe they want it, or they'd like to use it, but they don't want to own it.

If the voice rises on the words "a new home," the problem may be bigger than your phone call. The person obviously feels a great deal of financial pressure.

However, even if someone says something like that, it's not necessarily true. They may perceive it that way at that moment, but after talking to you for a few minutes, their perceptions could change.

One area where you need to be a little hard of hearing is when the prospect says no. "No" can mean many things; so can "yes."

You can't take what people say at face value. You have to look for the situation behind their words. How many of us would describe the same situation exactly the same way? Very few, I'd expect. But the way we choose to describe it reveals what we individually think is important.

To one person, when he or she says he or she wants a big house, uppermost in his or her mind could be all of the children having their own rooms. To another person, a big home could be a way to impress one's friends and co-workers. To someone else, owning a big home could be a sign that he or she has finally made it.

We may want the same things, but usually we want them for different reasons. By listening well, you'll discover those reasons — no matter what someone is saying.

Hand in hand with listening well goes not being afraid of silence. During any call, silence can be a wonderful way to cut through a maze of words and get to the heart of the matter.

Most of us don't like silence. We feel uncomfortable with it. But think of silence as your friend.

To a prospect, your silence is a reflection of understanding and patience.

Recognize the fact that some people find it difficult to answer questions. They may need a little time to come up with an answer. Give them that time. Don't interrupt. It's a mark of respect.

Only a big person knows how to give others the attention and concern we all crave. Listening well is not a passive activity. It's full of dynamics that can help your commissions grow.

During your calls, look for little verbal hints that tell you what the person on the other end of the line is like. Jot them down. File them away. And over time, you'll find you're becoming a pretty good judge of human character.

This is important, not only for showing your interest in your prospects, but also for yourself. The more you know about someone, the better you'll be able to guess at what point they'll enter the real estate market.

Don't worry about trying to carry on a brilliant conversation. Focus instead on learning to listen.

Helpful Transitions

Making smooth transitions, especially in response to a prospect's objections, is critical to successful farming by phone, because it enables us to link our thoughts together. It's amazing what one small word can do.

Words like, "understand," "appreciate," "agree," and "know" help make your phone conversations smoother. Note that all the words are positive and pleasant. Using words like these is vital if you want to come across as warm and friendly.

Other useful phrases include: "Sounds good, doesn't it?" and "What do you think?"

In addition, you'll want to weed the little negatives out of your speech — such as "don't understand," "dislike," "don't you know" — and you'll find them disappearing from your mind, too.

Summary

Questioning is a delicate art — a balancing act that draws a fine line between building a relationship and getting your point across.

Useful for softening the tone of a conversation, digging out relevant information, and steering the prospect toward where you want to go, your questions should begin right after you've captured a prospect's attention.

Socrates once said that you could accomplish more by asking people than by telling them, and it's true. Questions help in many ways. They:

1. Keep you out of arguments.
2. Prevent you from talking too much.
3. Help you get to know a prospect.
4. Help a prospect clarify his or her thinking.
5. Help people see what they really want.
6. Make a prospect feel important.

During your farming calls, you fall back on two types of questions: open-ended and closed-ended.

Open-ended questions leave a prospect room to respond. What to say is up to them. These questions start with words like "what" or "who" or the powerful "why." They're good for finding out more about the person you're talking to and for building rapport.

When you want more control over the conversation, turn to closed-ended questions. Often answered simply with a yes or no, questions like these come into play toward the end of the call when you're aiming at making a point.

Often telephone pros vary the types of questions they ask, giving a rhythm and pace to the call. Otherwise, a string of open-ended questions can sound like an interrogation, and a cluster of closed-ended ones makes you seem pushy.

Whatever types of questions you ask, there's one important thing to remember: Listen to the response. All too often we miss clues to how someone really feels and thinks because we take their words at face value. Tune in to the feeling behind the words and you'll be heading in the right direction.

Now let's move on to how to handle specific objections.

11. How to Handle Objections

The first and perhaps most important thing to remember about objections is that an objection is not the same as a rejection.

When someone raises an objection, you know you've gotten to first base. Why? Because they're willing to talk and to listen.

As we said earlier, hardly anyone will give you a flat no. Most people are too polite for that. So they lean on an excuse, or what you'd think of as an objection.

To the top real estate professionals, an objection is only someone saying, "You haven't convinced me yet. What else do you have to say?"

Remember, most of us were raised from childhood to resist any changes or new ideas that come our way. We like the status quo. We're comfortable with it. If it's going to change, someone is going to have to persuade us that making a change is in our best interest.

So don't be afraid when you sense a bit of resistance. Welcome the opportunity to try your hand at overcoming it.

The good things in life seldom come easily. View each challenge as a learning experience, a chance to grow personally and professionally. It's the people who overcome obstacles who make a success out of life.

Basic Guidelines

When it comes to handling an objection, don't forget that people may not remember what you said, but they'll never forget how you said it.

If there's even the slightest note of hostility in your voice, people will instantly pick it up.

Be pleasant, be positive, be a good conversationalist, and don't let any little negatives find their way into your words.

To see how positive a person you are, take a cassette recorder and tape a conversation with your husband or wife or your end of a telephone conversation with a friend.

Just listen to it once, and listen for all the negative words and phrases you use. Some people are negative all the time and they're not consciously aware of it.

But after awhile, often they find their friends turning away. That's because being around someone who's negative pulls you down. What you want is someone who lifts you up.

If you find you're more negative than you thought, start pausing a moment before you speak. Mentally switch gears and make the effort to look on the bright side.

When you're talking on the phone, the same principle applies. If you bad-mouth your competitors or are unfailingly critical, the only person they'll think poorly of is you.

When you hear an objection, often it's easier to respond on a negative note than a positive one. Avoid that temptation. One of the secrets of handling objections is to give the prospects the sense that they're being treated fairly. Fairness is something we all pick up intuitively.

If people have a sense they're being treated fairly, they'll be more willing to hear what you have to say.

That's also true if you give people choices. In our line of work, it's easy to try to make people's decisions for them. But that's the kiss of death.

Leave the choices up to them — and keep it that way, even when you're setting up the appointment at the end of a call. Let them pick the time. They'll feel more in control. And that's how you want them to feel, isn't it?

When you come head-to-head with an objection, there's a simple set of guidelines to follow. That may seem odd, but our minds do work in similar ways. Here they are:

1. Listen to the objection fully.
2. Repeat the objection back to the prospect.
3. If you don't understand it or you want more information, ask a question.
4. Respond to the objection.
5. Make sure the prospect understands your response.
6. Move right on.

One of the keys to handling objections is to answer them but don't miss a beat. Head right into the next benefit of what you're offering. That way, a prospect doesn't have time to keep digging into his objection. In a second, you're off to new ground.

The Six Most Common Objections

You probably think that if you make 300 calls, you'll run into 300 different reasons why people don't want what you're offering.
You're wrong. If you look at your Call Response Tally at the end of your farming by phone sessions, in the objections section, you'll see the same things said over and over again, just in different ways.

As varied as we are individually, we share a psychological makeup that we can never shed. People basically want the same things, with minor variations. No matter how unique we think we are, all of us try to meet certain fundamental needs.

Now let's twist that around. Just as we all have the same kinds of needs, we all raise the same types of objections when someone introduces change into our lives. The resistance that most of us have is incredible. But we can be persuaded, if the person we're talking to knows what he or she is doing.

Out of the hundreds of people you talk to, almost all of their objections will center around these six themes:

1. I can't afford it.
2. It's not what I want.
3. I already have an agent.
4. I have to talk it over with someone.
5. We want to do it ourselves.
6. I'm not interested.

These objections apply not only when you're showing a prospect specific houses; they also apply to any offer you make, even just the request for an appointment. People are so predictable, it's amazing. But don't take that for granted. If someone were calling you, you'd probably use one of those six objections, too.

If someone says, "I'm not interested," then slams down the phone — forget it. Make a note to call them back in a month or so. Don't throw their card away. You may have just caught them at a bad time.

If the person says, "I'm not interested" and stays on the line, the ball is in your court.

There is an art to dealing with objections. It runs contrary to all your natural instincts. You see, when someone disagrees with us, the first thing we want to do is tell them they're wrong. As a real estate professional, you can't do that — at least, not so they know what you're doing.

But there are ways to get people to see things differently — with new information, a change of perspective, or another angle.

When overcoming objections, you're not just trying to get people to change their minds. You want them to *reevaluate* the situation and *decide again,* based on whatever new slant you've been able to give them.

That may sound simplistic, but it implies a crucial difference in your attitude. If you're just trying to get someone to change his or her mind, you're thinking he or she is wrong. And the person will know that by your words.

If, on the other hand, you're trying to get them to reconsider something, you'll convey an element of personal concern that's lacking in the other approach.

Basically, in attempting to overcome objections, you're throwing out facts, testimonies, examples, and details that undermine the objections. But you're doing it with a positive spirit. And you use what the person tells you about himself or herself to structure your approach.

That's one reason why it's a good idea to start off

with open-ended questions.

Finding out what someone does for a living can be a key to what type of personality he or she is. So can knowing what clubs and groups the prospect belongs to. Or what the prospect does in his or her spare time.

In dealing with objections, you need to appeal to a prospect's own set of beliefs, values, standards, and intellect — not your own.

There are many ways to look at the world. Giving someone a little nudge to glance in another direction never hurts anyone.

Look for the Real Objection

As surprising as this sounds, the first objections people raise often are not the *real* objections.

You might be thinking, "Why would anyone lie?"

Well, it's not really a lie. Off the tops of their heads, they probably don't know what their real objections are. Or it may be a form of self-protection. We don't like to reveal too much about ourselves until we trust someone. Notice the word "trust" again?

To ferret out the true objection lurking behind the excuses, many professionals respond to an initial objection with a phrase like, "In addition to that, isn't there something else in the back of your mind?"

It's the second objection that is usually the genuine one. And when you recognize it, focus your attempts on overcoming it.

But remember, never let anyone know you think he or she is wrong — even about whether his or her own objection is a valid one.

The skillfulness of your questions and responses should let your prospects think they're figuring it out for themselves.

We all like to make our own decisions. Give your prospects that privilege.

Hit the "Hot Button"

All of us have fantasies of the home we'd like to own someday. Undoubtedly, many of these are rooted in childhood. If we grew up in the city, maybe we've always had a hankering for a yard full of shade trees. Or if the country was our childhood home, maybe it's thrilling for us to think of owning a penthouse suite.

If you can key into your prospects' dreams and figure out what really matters most to them, you'll go a long way toward closing a deal.

Once I had a young couple as clients, and though they never said so, each time I showed them a house with a pool, their eyes lit up. Of the original batch of listings I had to show them only two had pools. After finding this *hot button,* we switched gears and had them on their way.

All of us have secret hot buttons, things that trigger tides of memories, emotions, or dreams.

Maybe it's a father whose greatest desire in life is to leave something tangible to his children. Or a woman who has always wanted to live in the most exclusive section of town. Or someone who fantasizes about a house hidden at the end of a long, curved driveway.

It doesn't take hours of conversation to figure out what people really want. Sometimes you'll know in the first few minutes of a call — that is, if you ask the right questions and give your full attention to the answers.

Phrases That Turn an Objection Around

When you respond to objections effectively, you can turn negative factors into positive ones. Remember, it's all in how we see it. There was a woman I heard about whose husband drove her crazy. Every night he would go methodically through the house, checking every single door and window to make sure they were locked. He did this even if his wife had just locked them. Finally, she couldn't stand it anymore. How could anyone live with a man who was so picky?

But then she realized that his finickiness was what had taken him so far in the business world. As the president of a bank, he had to be careful with details. The characteristic that drove her nuts was the secret of his success.

Once she saw it that way, his fanatical locking up of the house never bothered her again.

To turn a negative into a positive, to twist around an objection, you don't need a laundry list of possible responses. But you do need to clue in to what a prospect is really saying, and you need a few all around answers that help you take the wind out of objections.

More often than not, the same objection a prospect gives to cut you off can be used as the main reason he or she should take you up on your offer.

The rationale, I suppose, is that by discovering someone's true objection, we find out what their primary motivator is. Knowing that tells us what approach to use. And chances are that the prospect has no idea he or she has given us such valuable information.

In handling objections, there are a few good phrases that work magic.

"Feel, Felt , Found"

These three little words are one of the salesperson's oldest and dearest friends. In fact, they've probably been over used. But they carry a feeling you'll want to stay close to.

Suppose a prospect said, "I'd love to own a new home. But we just can't afford it right now."

Using "feel, felt, found," you'd say, "I know how you feel. Many people have felt that way. But with the new kinds of financing now available, people have found they can afford houses they could only dream of owning before."

This approach makes a prospect feel he or she isn't the only one who has had this type of problem. Others have had it, too. And, as the agent points out, they've discovered something that helped them rise above it.

Little "Yes's" Lead the Way

Running into a stone wall of sales resistance, the best way to break it down is by chipping away at the edges. Hitting it head-on is useless — you'll only wind up with a skull fracture.

But if you start courting a reluctant prospect, getting them to agree with you on minor points, by the time you reach the major point, the prospect is much more inclined to go along with you. Here's an example:

Prospect: I've had this home for five years and I'm not about to sell it now.

Agent: But, Mr. Hoskins, wouldn't your family enjoy living in a more spacious home?

194

Prospect: I suppose so.

Agent: Couldn't you use some extra room?

Prospect: Yes.

Agent: If moving into a larger home could wind up saving you money over the next few years, wouldn't you be interested? You are interested in saving money, aren't you?

Prospect: Isn't everybody?

Agent: Mr. Hoskins, I'd be happy to show you a way you and your family could . . .

By stringing along the questions, the agent keeps drawing the prospect out, getting him or her to agree, until the prospect can come to only one conclusion — one based not on opinion or hearsay, but on solid facts.

The next time someone raises an objection, try passing it right back to them with a question. Then keep the questions coming until finally they see the light.

Questions often help prospects realize that their objections are of no consequence after all. Using this approach helps prospects work out in their own minds why they should meet with you. It's gentle, friendly, and it works. Remember, let little "yes's" pave your way to a successful close.

"If You Were"

If you take the "if you were" tack, one thing you better be sure of is that you are 100% sincere. Otherwise, you'll not only fail, you'll also eliminate your chance to try again.

Probably better than anything else, this approach epitomizes the real estate pro who genuinely cares about his prospects and wants only to do what's best for them.

When you hit a major roadblock, and you know that what you're suggesting will truly make the prospect's life better, then try this approach:

Agent   Mrs. Frankel, if you were my own mother, I'd say to you what I'm saying now. There is no better investment for anyone today than owning their own home.

Take that approach with absolute sincerity, and if your prospect doesn't do an about-face then and there, you can be sure that at least you've given them something they'll seriously think about. In addition, using this approach goes a long way toward building up a prospect's trust in you.

"In Many Cases"

The phrase "in many cases" is not one of my personal favorites. It's often used with a note of superiority that I dislike.

A gentler version of it goes like this:

Prospect: It's impossible for me to get a decent house with monthly payments as low as my rent is now.

Agent: In many cases, I'd have to agree with you. But there is a new program, offered by the state of California, only for first-time home buyers . . .

Using the transition "in many cases" softens the agent's objection, making it easier for the prospect to agree. For example, the agent could have responded with this:

Agent: But didn't you know that the state of California is offering special rates to first-time home buyers?

Although the prospect may be interested in the program, his irritation at being told he's stupid undoubtedly will outweigh whatever interest he has.

In both cases, the same information is offered. The first case, though, is wrapped in a more attractive package.

Using phrases such as "in many cases" or "under different circumstances" or "normally" creates a receptivity to what you're going to say next. These phrases give the prospect credit for thinking the way he or she does. Most important of all, they take the harsh edges off of your words.

Other Important Phrases

"In many cases" deserved a heading of its own. But like the phrases that follow, it is a transition used to lead into a head-on response to an objection or to sidestep it and move to another benefit of your offer.

Transitions help a conversation flow more naturally by building bridges between thoughts. Use them often and you'll find they make your job a lot easier. It's a good feeling to be nice to people and words like these help you do it:

"You are right, of course, but have you ever thought that . . . ?"

"Naturally, you have a choice . . ."

"What you're really saying is that you are interested, just not right now. Is that right?"

"I know that you only want to do what's best for you and your family. Have you ever considered . . . ?"

"The Jones family was in a situation similar to yours. But they realized that . . ."

This kind of language encourages empathy between you and your prospect, putting yourself in his or her shoes — seeing things from his or her point of view.

Responses That Keep You on Track

In this section, we're going to cover a host of objections and give you some suggestions on how to handle them.

What's important aren't the words themselves, but a pattern of thinking. It won't take you long to catch on to how to turn a negative into a positive and move smoothly to the next thought.

"I Can't Afford It"

When you hear those four words, get ready. The prospect is telling you he wants it and either he isn't sure it's worth what someone is asking or he has doubts about how he can pay for it.

If he questions the price, you can talk about the quality of the home, compare it to what other homes in the same neighborhood are selling for, or review the upward trend in prices over the past year. Other things you may want to mention include: terms, financing, special features, tax advantages, the excellent location, good schools, and nearby parks. Here you're showing the prospect that there are reasons for the price — good reasons.

Or you could take another tack and throw in comments like:

> *"Doesn't your family deserve a house like this? Don't you, too?"*

> *"You get what you pay for"* (a lesson we've all learned at some time in our lives).

> *"This kind of house isn't for everybody."*

> *"Think of it as an investment, and look at how this house will appreciate over the next few years."*

If money is the problem, break the price down. If the prospect's upper limit is $150,000 and his wife is captivated by a $160,000 home, break down the $10,000 into how much more he'd be paying a month.

If it's $50, then multiply it out to a year. Ask "Couldn't you afford $600 a year for a home twice as large as the one you have now?" Or "Isn't it worth $50 a month to keep your family really happy?" Make it easy for him to buy.

One tip, when it comes to numbers, is to let the prospect figure it out for himself. Even over the phone, you can ask him to get a pencil and paper and do the math. Participating this way seems to give people a more personal stake in the conversation, and it also keeps them in line with your thinking.

"I Need to Think It Over"

How many times have you heard this line? More often than not, many people respond with something like, "That's fine, Miss Emery. If you change your mind, you have my number." The trouble with that response is that the salesperson has lost control. At the very least, you want to keep the initiative and set up a time to call back in two days.

When people say they need time to think about it, they could be reluctant to tell you their real objections. Thinking things over has been an excuse since the beginning of time.

Sometimes people mean it, but often it's just a way of trying to politely end the call. If you think that's what they're doing, try to find out their real objections.

Another choice is to agree with them that this is an important decision that needs a lot of thought. Then review how what you're offering can help them. By going over the same ground, you may find them more willing to tell you the truth.

Personally, I prefer a slightly different approach. When people say they want to think it over, I offer to help them do it.

Your response might go like this: "Mr. Galloway, I can understand that. Selling your home is a big step. But wouldn't it help you to know what the market in this area is like today and what people are getting for similar houses right in your own neighborhood? I'd be happy to bring that information to your home tonight. What time is better for you, seven or eight o'clock?"

Another response to a prospect who wants to think it over could be to emphasize that timing is critical. If you're offering a Home-Protection Kit, remind them that they only have two more weeks to get one. If it's a home market analysis, you may want to focus on how quickly the market is changing, or how they should take advantage of mortgage rates that are lower than they've been in five years.

"I'm Not in the Market Right Now"

As you can probably guess, this objection demands another "timing is critical" response. One thing working in your favor is the fact that housing prices seldom go down.

It's easy for you to get past records on what the average home in your area has sold for over the past ten years, and you can trace the upward spiral for a prospect.

"There's no better time than now" is a line that's almost always true in our business. If mortgage rates are currently high, they can always refinance later. But the longer they wait, the more it's going to cost them to buy.

When the market goes up, they'll also probably make more money on selling their home. But they'll have to buy one, too. And nobody wants to pay any more than they have to.

"I Have to Talk It Over with Someone"

Here again, stress how critical timing is in such a fast-moving market. You can also do a variation on the response to the "think it over " objection, by offering to bring over materials that will help them fully understand the situation. Offer to meet with them, but keep your voice casual, friendly, and wanting only to help, so they don't feel as if you're pushing them into a meeting.

"I Already Have a Real Estate Agent"

You probably won't hear this line very often, because most people think of a relationship with a real estate agent as temporary — something which, by the way, you're trying to eliminate with farming by phone. The reason most people lose touch with their agents is because most salespeople never follow up. Once a deal is over, the client is forgotten.

However, there are times when you may call someone who already has a relationship with another agent or company.

When that happens, don't give up right away. And don't you dare say anything negative about whomever they're talking about. Praise your competitors and people will trust you. But then point out what you have to offer right at that moment.

Once, when I was looking for a house, I had an agent who specialized in the area where I wanted to live. But I wasn't happy with her. I called other agents, even met with them, and not one followed through with me. If they had, I would gladly have switched agents. But I don't think any of them really listened to me or tried to understand me. All they were thinking was, Is he serious about this or not? I was, and I told them so, but they didn't hear me. So they never called.

Emphasize what you can do for a prospect right then. Maybe it's to show them property that evening. Talk about what you can do that others can't. Maybe your company is a full-service real estate brokerage that can handle financing, too.

When you farm, you have an advantage because you specialize in that neighborhood. If the prospect is thinking of selling, stress the fact that you have a group of buyers looking exclusively in that area.

Tell your prospects what makes you unique.

One final note: If the person you call has already listed with another agent, back off. And then wait and see if it expires.

"Send Me Some Information to Look At"

When you hear this, it's a golden opportunity to ask questions:

"Would you like a brochure on what services we offer?"

"Can I mail you information on recent sales in your neighborhood?"

From these nuts-and-bolts questions, you can then move on to more personal ground and try to get at why he or she wants the information.

If they don't tell you, that's okay. Get the information in the mail right away and call them back two or three days later. Then you'll have another chance to find out where they're coming from.

"You'd Be Wasting Your Time"

The words sound harsh, but you can give a gentle response. "Mr. Gregg, I'd be happy to give up a few minutes of my time if it means helping you and your family make thousands of dollars in the coming years. Making money is important to you, isn't it?"

"I Don't Need a New Home"

Well, they may not need one, but chances are they'd like one. Being content is a state of mind few of us are fortunate enough to experience.

When you hear this, try the little "yes's":

> *"But wouldn't you like more room? Or a bigger kitchen? Perhaps another bedroom? What about a fireplace to keep you warm in winter?"*

If you keep trying, people will respect you. I know I've bought tons of cleaning solution I didn't need simply because the salesperson did such a good job. People don't mind if you're forceful. They do mind if you're aggressive. Keep a delicate balance.

For Sale By Owner (FSBO)

The minute a homeowner puts up a "for sale by owner" (FSBO) sign in his or her front yard, the phone will begin to ring. Most of the calls, however, will not be from prospective buyers, but rather from realtors looking for the listing.

One of the first things many agents do in the morning is scan through the classified ads looking for FSBO ads.

So when you make an FSBO call, keep in mind that you will not be the first. Moreover, to break through the clutter, you need to be unique.

The FSBO Kit

One approach I've seen used successfully is to prepare a For Sale By Owner Kit — which might include tips for preparing an open house, ad writing, signs, and other pointers for the prospect.

Then instead of jumping all over the homeowner

trying to get a listing, offer to drop the kit off at the prospect's house, thus beating the crowd of realtors by getting your foot in the door — with an open invitation from the homeowner.

The Commission Objection

Beyond the FSBO Kit approach, you can take the head-on tack. In this case, you might respond with something like this:

"Mrs. Foster, when someone says that to me, I know it's because either they had a bad experience with a real estate broker in the past or because they're hoping to save the commissions. Would you mind telling me if either is true for you?"

If it's the first, of course, you'd sympathize and gently throw in that not every agent is like that. If they think the commission isn't worth it, here's a list of reasons you can use to handle the commission objection:

1. The classic: The seller doesn't pay the commission, the buyer does.
2. When you sell your own home, you attract hordes of bargain hunters. These people have many homes to choose from. You have only yours to sell. That doesn't put you in a very good position for negotiating.
3. It's hard to negotiate a deal for your own home because of your emotional involvement. You may think that your home is worth more because of certain features you love, but buyers in today's market won't pay for those features.

4. When you sell your own home, you get calls and visitors 24 hours a day. People are forever dropping by to see your property. It quickly becomes a great nuisance. Also you're advertising your phone number for all the world to see.
5. Real estate transactions are complicated, with many legal requirements and long processes. It takes someone who knows the field well to properly handle and check all the paperwork. A missed deadline or forgotten bank statement can easily cause a deal to fall through.
6. There are many ways to handle real estate financing. Only an expert knows them all and knows which one is best in a given situation.

The Advantages of Listing with a Broker

1. We screen prospective buyers, bringing only qualified buyers to your home.
2. We take a professional picture of your home and prepare a detailed profile that we give to every interested prospect.
3. We handle showing the home, so there is no inconvenience to you. We let you know in advance when someone is coming to see it, and we work within your schedule.
4. We write and place advertisements in newspapers and magazines for you. It doesn't cost you anything.
5. We sponsor open houses and special showings.
6. We already have in our files a list of people interested in homes in your area.

7. We can handle the entire back end: helping to arrange financing, making sure escrow is proceeding smoothly, keeping everything on schedule.

One agent working the floor got a call from a man planning to sell his own home. He wanted information as to how much other people were getting for their homes in his area.

Apparently, he had called a number of different real estate companies and gotten the cold shoulder. However, this agent took the trouble to look up the prices and call the man back. They had a long and pleasant conversation.

The man was so impressed that now he's a client of the agent's. No, he didn't give the agent the listing. But the agent is helping his family look for a new home.

And the agent is getting a fee for helping with the paperwork when the home is sold.

Dead Ends

There are people you have to give up on. Not forever, but for awhile. If someone is running through four or five objections and you try to argue each one, forget the appointment. Instead, be quiet and let the person ramble on. Eventually he or she will settle on the point that's most important. Then you can deal with it.

If it's a whole list of excuses that doesn't seem to be going anywhere, politely end the call, and call back in a few months with a different offer.

Occasionally, you'll run into someone who's really having a hard time financially or who is unemployed. You'll be surprised at how open people can be about things like that right at the beginning of a call. Believe them. Call back in six months.

Summary

Now we're getting into the nitty-gritty of specific responses to objections. First, though, came the reminder that an objection does not equal rejection. Often an objection can be interpreted as someone saying, "You haven't persuaded me yet, keep talking."

Although objections come in many shapes and sizes, they all revolve around central themes. Basically, these are:

- I can't afford it
- I don't want it
- I already have an agent
- I have to talk it over with someone
- I want to do it myself
- I'm not interested

In more than half the calls you make, the first objection you hear will not be the real one. Pay closer attention to the second one; usually it's the truth.

As for how to handle objections, we ran through several pages of examples. Knowing how to overcome objections isn't a matter of memorizing phrases. It's more a way of thinking that softens resistance, makes prospects feel important, gives them credit for their feelings, and gently glides to a close.

We also reviewed a number of approaches to take when you run up against people who want to sell their houses themselves.

Finally, there are dead ends. But a dead end today

may not be one tomorrow. People change and so do their circumstances.

12. The Critical Close

When you're about to close, you're ready to move into the home stretch. You've managed to put the objections aside, the prospect seems to agree with your point of view, there's a stir of interest, and a taste of desire. What do you do next?

First of all, you don't rush. Too many sales professionals try to run a prospect down with a steamroller. Or even worse, they never nail anything down.

Basically, closing is asking someone to take action. In your case, when you're farming by phone, it's the request to set up an appointment.

In classified sales ads, you'll often see companies looking for people who "know how to close."

Closing isn't a natural ability. It's something you learn how to do. When you attempt to close, all those hours of thinking about your script, writing it, rehearsing it, using it — that's when they pay off.

Each close is a moment of truth.

But don't be fooled. Remember that even the world's greatest salespeople hardly ever close on their first attempt. Usually it's the fifth.

Every commission you earn is won by a series of closings. First it's the appointment. Then signing a listing. Or showing properties. Then an offer. Maybe another offer. Then a contract. Then the end of escrow.

Closing a deal is something you do step-by-step. When you think of it that way, it's easier to handle. And it puts the importance where it belongs.

Don't rush into your closes; but don't keep stringing along the conversation, waiting for the prospect to suggest a meeting.

Closing is something that should come naturally. Don't force it. Don't delay it.

One thing to remember from the moment you dial the phone is to never, never appear over anxious. That attitude only alerts a prospect to the fact that you care more about yourself than you do him or her.

Convey a Sense of Urgency

Every effort at closing needs one characteristic: a sense of urgency.

That's true for all areas of direct marketing. We can talk until we're blue in the face and we can ask people to act, but we have to give them a reason to do it *now*.

I've seen more telephone scripts and direct mail letters fail from a lack of urgency than for any other reason.

If people feel they can put something off, especially a big decision involving their home, they will. You need to develop a special sensitivity in this area because our natural tendency is to not want to force people into doing something.

You can't think of it that way. What you're doing is helping people make decisions that will benefit their lives and their families' lives for years to come.

If they don't do it now, when will they?

What you use to create that sense of urgency will depend on your offer.

Occasionally, agents or finance companies offer free appraisals, if someone lists or buys a home through them. And the offer is good only for a limited time.

Other elements that add urgency: a sharp drop in mortgage rates (that may not last), a special financing package, changes in the tax law (so you'd better act before the end of the year), or the quick average turnover on homes.

Wherever time comes into play, there's a place for the message, "If you don't act now, you'll be missing a great opportunity."

In reviewing your script, always check for a sense of urgency.

When to Close

There's no magical formula for determining the best time to go for the close. Sometimes you try as soon as you've finished the reason for the call, before they have a chance to respond. Sometimes you wait.

If you do it too soon, you could seem overeager. On the other hand, you're letting someone know where the conversation is going. That can help.

Some sales whizzes recommend putting off any attempts to close until after you've finished dealing with all the objections. In some cases, that could be quite awhile.

Others believe in ignoring objections until you've wrapped up your presentation and asked for an appointment.

The route you choose will depend on you and on the type of person you're talking to.

You can't even pin it down by the personality type of your prospect. Sometimes, when you're dealing with curt and to-the-point people, it's best to follow their example and spell things out right away. Other times, you should try to break through that efficiency barrier and find the real person.

It's a matter of developing the right intuition on how to handle each moment. Some of that you can learn from books; some can only come from experience.

Whenever you start to close, you can be almost sure you'll have to do it more than once. So have in mind a few ways of asking the same thing. You don't want to sound repetitious. It's simple, really, to change things around.

Maybe the first time you say, "I'll be in your neighborhood later this week, and I'd love to stop by. Which day would be best for you, Thursday or Friday?"

The second time, try "If I stop by on Thursday, about 3 p.m., will you have a couple of minutes to go over this, or would 4 p.m. be better?"

On the third attempt, try "I'd be happy to show you some comparable homes right in your own area. What day is better for you, Thursday or Friday?"

Just be careful about getting one line stuck in your head and falling back on it all the time. That's unpleasant for the person who's listening.

How to Close Effectively

I've read a thousand and one ways to close. They're called everything from "The Presidential Close" to "The Puppy Dog Close." Unfortunately, most of the names don't give you a hint as to how to do it.

The variations are endless. But, frankly, you can boil closes down to a few techniques.

Direct Close

Most sales pros would tell you to stay away from this one. You're giving the prospect too much room to maneuver. Use a direct close only when you're sure the prospect is in your hip pocket and he or she will agree to anything.

Here are a few examples:

"Would you like me to stop by this evening?"

"Don't you think it would help if I could show you what's available?"

"Would you be interested in sitting down with me and figuring out if this is the best move for you?"

In all three of these cases, you're laying yourself wide open to the possibility that the prospect will say no. In fact, you're making it easy for him or her to say no. Many real estate professionals avoid this approach at all costs.

Assumptive Close

Now you just *assume* that the prospect has decided to meet with you. You go on with the conversation as though the decision has been made, finalizing the details.

This technique is better than the direct close because it assumes the positive. But some people find it offensive. They like to be the ones making the decisions.

With an assumptive close, you might say something like this:

"What time would you like me to stop by?"

"When can I show you what's available?"

"Are you interested in seeing what land is selling for, as well as houses in the area?"

"How soon can we get together?"

If you misread a client's signals and he's not willing to meet with you when you use an assumptive close, he has to speak up and say you're wrong. That's hard for a lot of people to do.

Sometimes they'll meet with you, just to avoid a confrontation.

Forced-Choice Close

Sales experts the world over praise the *forced-choice close*. With it, you not only assume the prospect will meet with you, in the same breath you give them the chance to make a decision. Whichever they choose, the close goes through.

Throughout this book, all the closes you've seen have been forced-choice closes. Recognize them?

"I'll be in your neighborhood tonight. What time would you prefer I stop by — seven o'clock? Or is eight o'clock better for you?"

"What area would you like to see — Brook-haven, Ridgeside, or both?"

"Which day is better for you to come to my office, Wednesday or Thursday?"

"Would you like to drop by my office, or is it more convenient if I come to your home?"

Using this type of close, you can still be professional and direct, but warm. People don't see you as pushy, but as someone who lets them make their own decisions. And that's what they want to do.

The three approaches we've just outlined are the standard models. You can dress them up, add a little glitter. But when you get right down to it, psychologically those are the elements you'll deal with.

However, you should be aware of some variations that can get you out of a pinch. Many of these have been developed for face-to-face meetings, but they can easily be adapted for use over the phone.

Ben Franklin Approach

Some people simply can't think unless they write things down. We all know people who have endless lists, writing down pros and cons, helping them make their decisions.

If you've hit a brick wall, regroup. Ask the prospect to jot a few things down. Start off with all the reasons why he *shouldn't* meet with you. You've already heard all of those in his objections.

When he's finished, have him draw a line down the middle of the page. On the other half, write down all the reasons why he *should* meet with you.

Of course, the reasons why he or she should meet with you will be greater in number and weight than the reasons why not.

By the time the prospect is done, what he or she should do will be right there on the piece of paper.

Another "Yes"

This is something to think about. I've had people use it on me and it works. Basically, it's a variation of the assumptive close.

It goes like this: "I can stop by your house Monday afternoon, about three o'clock, I think. You will be home Monday, won't you?"

Before they know what's happening, they've said yes. What you've done is immediately divert their attention from the fact that you're assuming they'll meet with you. Without pausing for even a second, you've tossed in a harmless little question to which they're almost sure to answer yes. Afterward, it's hard for them to backtrack.

Last Ditch

Here you throw caution to the wind. You know you've lost. You're giving up. But the prospect has been friendly and you still have a slim hope. So with a note of sadness and self-incrimination in your voice, you plaintively ask, "Mr. Elkhart, what did I do wrong?"

Now the prospect wants to help you. In doing so, chances are they'll open up far more readily than they did when they were the ones in the spotlight.

Once this happens, you're on your way.

What About Your Friends?

This is another sign of resignation. You won't get anywhere with this prospect. You feel it in your bones. But it has been a pleasant conversation. Before writing him off entirely, ask if any of his friends or relatives would like to live in the area. Or ask if any of his neighbors are thinking of selling their homes.

Talk a little bit about how you specialize in the prospect's area, how you're always on the lookout for new listings or prospective buyers, and that you'd appreciate whatever help he could give you.

You never know what kind of response you'll get. Maybe he's the president of the local country club, with lots of contacts. Or the head of a nearby union with many members who live in your farm. Or a schoolteacher who knows hundreds of families.

One thing everybody talks about is their plans for buying, selling, or building a home. Following up a few friendly tips could easily lead to some hefty commissions.

The Finishing Touch

Each time you attempt to close, you're at a crossroad. One fork leads to an appointment; the other leads nowhere. What happens at the close can put you on either path — or you can stay right where you are. Sometimes you may even feel as if you're taking a few steps backward.

The close is a point of decision. The prospect weighs your reasons and, consciously or unconsciously, chooses a course of action.

It's at this time that a prospect needs reassurance. Whenever we make a decision, we worry about three things:

- Whether it's okay for us to do it
- Whether the decision is sound
- Whether others will think it's okay, too

Even if the conversation has gone so well that there's no question in your mind that the prospect's interested, still give him or her that psychological pat on the back.

Phrases like these will do it:

"You'll find that knowing what houses are selling for right in your own neighborhood will really help you determine the value of your home."

"With the market as strong as it is today, you're considering a move at just the right time."

"You'll be pleasantly surprised when you see how much your home has appreciated over the past five years."

At the end of a call, all too often salespeople drop the ball. As soon as they hear a yes, they give a mental sigh of relief and drop the courtesies. Now they're just anxious to finalize the appointment and move on. All the caring leaves their voice.

Top salespeople know the secret of their success is genuine concern for their clients. They don't use kindness manipulatively.

If you ruin the last 15 seconds of your call by taking off the cloak of courtesy, the prospect may meet with you — once. Or they may call and cancel.

Remember, the close of a call is just as important as its beginning. Be consistent in your approach. And you'll see consistent results.

A Word of Caution

During a call, you take so much care to avoid being misinterpreted. You also have to watch that you don't misinterpret your prospect.

If someone asks, "Could we have our home in the Multiple Listing Book by Friday?" don't assume that's what they want. Ask them, "Would you like to have your home in the Multiple Listing Book by Friday?"

In our line of work, it's important to have good communication in both directions. If you misinterpret people, they might think you're not too bright. Keep things clear and aboveboard, and everybody will be happy.

Summary

The close is the bottom line of the farming phone call. It's the decisive moment when you ask for the appointment.

You can try to close at the beginning, middle, or end of your call. Wherever you do it, though, make sure you add a sense of urgency. If you don't give people a reason to act now, they'll delay indefinitely — especially when it comes to a major decision like buying or selling a home.

More people in sales fail because they don't know how to close than for any other reason. Closing is not a natural ability. It's a skill you learn through practice. If you think of it as trying to force people to do something, you'll never make it. Instead think of closing as asking them to take the first step along a path that will make their lives better.

Essentially, there are three ways for you to ask for an appointment:

Direct Close — The least favorite of them all, this approach makes it easy for a prospect to turn you down. You put the whole ball game in his or her lap by asking something like, "Do you want to meet with me?" It's rather like starting off the conversation with "Do you want to sell your house?" You should banish both phrases from your vocabulary.

Assumptive Close — A bit better than the direct close, in the assumptive mode you assume the prospect has said yes. So you proceed to nail down the details as though everything has been resolved. Here you run the risk of a prospect correcting you with, "But I never said I wanted to meet with you. Where did you get that idea?" It's better to let the prospect make some sort of a decision.

Forced-Choice Close — The best of all. Now the prospect feels as though he or she is making the decision. But you structure it so that either choice he or she makes, you're going to meet. Here you assume he's agreed to an appointment and you let him pick the day, time, or place. This approach drastically cuts down the chance of a no, while making the prospect feel he or she has had a say in things.

If you're really stuck at the end of a call, there are other attempts you can make to salvage the conversation before the final close.

You can try the Ben Franklin approach, where the prospect *writes down* all the pros and cons of

221

meeting with you; the last ditch approach, where you sadly ask, "What did I do wrong?"; the "another yes," where you set up the appointment, then quickly follow with a question they have to answer yes to; or finally, if all else fails, you can ask if they know someone in the market to buy or sell a home.

When you finish the close, remember to reassure the prospect that what he or she is doing is the right thing.

13. Wrapping It Up

When you've finished the close, here's a tip: Be quiet. Sometimes, when the tension disappears, we have a tendency to relax and let words spill out of our mouths. But here it's more important than ever for you to stay professional.

As soon as you've gotten an appointment or you've decided to hang it up for now, move smoothly into the wrap-up. This stage of the call is as critical as any other.

Good-Bye Is Not Forever

I don't think there will be a single time when you end a call and say, "Thank heavens; that's the last time I'll have to deal with him." In this line of work, that seldom happens.

Never knowing what the future will bring, you can't afford to offend anyone. Someone who moves away from your farm could move back a year later.

If you just don't like someone, work at liking him or her. You may be surprised at how your feelings can change.

People are your business. You can't afford to

write off anybody.

With that behind us, let's get into the specific steps to go through when finalizing a call. If the prospect has agreed to meet with you, you need to:

1. Set up the specifics of the appointment (date, time, and place).
2. Repeat the specifics.
3. Give the prospect your name and phone number.
4. Thank them for their time and patience.
5. Be the last to hang up.

More often, of course, you'll have established the beginnings of a relationship, but the stage isn't set yet for a meeting. Then the wrap up might go like this:

1. Summarize the outcome of the call.
2. Tell them you'll be calling again and give an approximate date.
3. Thank them for their time and patience.
4. Be the last to hang up.

Setting Up the Appointment

When it comes to setting up an appointment, it's best to schedule it as soon as possible. That way the positive feelings from your call will linger. Some real estate professionals, though, prefer to schedule all their appointments for the next week, so they can start off Monday morning with maximum efficiency. Do whatever feels best for you.

Sometimes you may want prospects to meet you at your office, where you can feel more in charge and more professional. But most often, you should meet prospects in their homes.

Being willing to drive to people's homes says that they're important to you. It shows the personal attention you give every person you help. That one gesture will set you apart from most other agents.

It can also be useful to you because you'll see how your prospects live. And that will tell you a lot about the kind of people they are.

Once I heard a building contractor talking about how he could walk into someone's house and, in a few minutes, tell you what kind of music they listened to, what kind of car they drove, how often they did their laundry, and whether they watched a lot of TV. Our homes are windows through which others see us.

Ultimately, the decision on where to meet should belong to the prospect. Whatever they choose, let them know you'll do everything you can to make the meeting happen. It starts with a willingness to bend your schedule to fit their schedule.

Not long ago, I met a former top Cadillac salesman in California. His secret? Whenever he sold a car, he'd call the new owners three months later, reminding them it was time for a checkup. The next morning, he'd be at their house, drop off his Cadillac, and drive theirs to the dealership. That night he'd bring it back, all tuned up and ready to go.

After a few months, he had so many referrals he had trouble handling them. By then, people were calling up, and he was selling cars over the phone. He'd ask what they wanted, they'd work out a deal and that night, he'd be on their doorstep, keys in hand.

Sounds incredible, doesn't it? But people liked the fact that he went to such lengths to make them happy. These days, it's unusual to find people who show that much concern for you.

So let your prospects know that you value their time and their willingness to see you. Even if you've proved beyond a shadow of a doubt that it's in their own interest to do so.

Do anything to meet them, and you'll find them meeting you more than halfway.

Write It Down, Please

When we're talking, we want to feel as if our listener is hanging on our every word. The truth is, they only pay attention to one out of every ten words. That means the chances are great they'll miss our name or the time of the appointment or the place where we're meeting.

When giving instructions over the phone, you can't be too careful. If there's a mistake, you don't want to waste your time waiting for someone to show up or knocking on an unanswered door. Time is money, you know.

So make sure you repeat everything. Ask the prospect if he or she has a pencil and paper. Make sure he or she writes everything down.

The same goes for you, too. As you're setting up an appointment, be writing it in your schedule book.

If it's set for the prospect's home, verify the address — even though it's on the index card in front of your face. It could be a number or two off. The last thing you want to do is walk up to the wrong house and be embarrassed. It'll start your meeting off poorly, especially if your prospects see you doing it.

When you're writing down the appointment in your book, it's also a good idea to write instructions next to it. That way, the next time you go back, you don't have to worry about finding a little scrap of paper, and you don't have to ask again.

Also remember to give the prospects your name and a phone number where they can reach you if something comes up.

If the meeting is at your office, ask if they know how to get there. If there's any doubt at all on the directions, go through them step-by-step. If they get lost, you both lose time.

Say It Again

One of the cardinal rules for any sales or direct marketing effort is this sequence:

- Tell them what you're going to tell them
- Tell them
- Tell them what you've just told them

Repetition may seem to be the mother of boredom, but it's also the route to success in sales. People don't always take in what we're saying right away. As the conversation continues, they think about what we're saying. After they've heard it enough times, they begin to believe it.

Post-Close, Follow-up Questions

Once the appointment is set, it's a good time to ask a few more questions. If you haven't asked how many people are in the family, do it now. Or inquire about what they do for a living. Don't go overboard with your questions or they'll get annoyed. Just ask about the basics so you can think about them and make specific recommendations during the meeting.

If it has been a pleasant conversation but they're

not ready to see you, let them know that you'll be calling again. That will be a sign that you're serious about your work and your commitment to their neighborhood.

You don't have to give them a specific time frame. Just say something like, "Well, I'll be calling back in a few months or so, just to see if anything has changed." Hardly anyone will tell you not to bother. Remember, in this business, good-bye is never forever.

Showing Your Gratitude

After the appointment is set, the directions confirmed, the psychological pat on the back given, isn't it time to hang up?

Not yet.

As the courteous person that you are, there's one more important thing you need to do.

You need to say *thank-you.*

It doesn't matter if you consider the call a success or not. That person has been willing to listen to you and talk to you. He or she is entitled to your gratitude.

If you've run into one of those desperately lonely types who've poured out their heart, or if someone has shared information with you that could be considered confidential, thank them for their confidence. Let them know they can trust you.

However, on every call, you can always thank the listener for his or her time and patience. Then you can add, "I look forward to meeting you." Or "I look forward to talking to you again."

These thank-yous carry a lot of weight — not because what they say is so important — but because people will remember that you were nice to them.

228

It's through common courtesies that we leave our mark. Overlook them, and people will overlook you. Once again, be the last to hang up. Wait for the click in your ear to tell you the call is over. If someone has a last-minute thought, there's nothing more frustrating than talking into a dead phone line. And no one will go to the trouble of looking up your number and calling you back.

Our minds don't always work as readily as our mouths. Give people the opportunity for a last-minute change of heart. You never know when it'll happen.

Filing a Reminder

As you're placing the phone back in its cradle, decide then and there when you'll call again.

If you decide to shuffle it into the next time you make farming calls for that area, note that on the prospect's card.

One way to do that is by using small, colored adhesive circles. If you're breaking up your farming by phone into four calls a year to each home, you may want to set up a system like this:

Blue stickers	Winter
Yellow stickers	Spring
Green stickers	Summer
Orange stickers	Fall

If you're bumping someone from your winter session to your spring session, just stick a yellow circle on his or her card.

If you decide you need to call back in a few weeks, set a specific date and write it down in your schedule book.

Do this before moving on to the next call. All you need to jot down is their name. Before you call, you'll want to pull out the card with the number anyway, just to refresh your memory.

Or you may prefer to write a note to yourself and stick it in your chronological file under the appropriate date. Do whatever works best for you.

During the entire conversation, you should be making brief notes on the prospect's card, describing what objections they raise and your impressions of them. Check to make sure you can read what you've written. If you can't, fix it. It won't be any easier in a few months.

If you've filled in any of the lines on the front of the Manual Farm Form, make sure you did it properly.

Occasionally, you'll run into a prospect you hit it off with immediately. Or a call was so positive, even if they didn't agree to an appointment, that you want to follow up.

For calls like those, sending a short thank-you note or writing a special handwritten message on your next direct-mail letter might be appropriate.

If you decide a thank-you note is in order, set the prospect's card aside and write it as soon as you finish your farming session on the phone. Be sure it gets in the mail that day.

If you opt for a handwritten message, make a note and put it in a file you keep just for that purpose. That way, every time you're ready to mail out a bunch of letters, you can check in the file for which ones need special attention.

Finally, if you've promised to send out some information, do it as soon as your phone farming session is over, and enclose a little note. Then write down in your schedule book to call them in two or three days to see if they've gotten your material and what they think of it.

Please don't forget to write everything down. You may think you have the memory of an elephant, especially at the time you're making a decision. But even elephants forget.

Moving On

When the call is over and the paperwork is done, what's next?

Whatever you do, don't take a coffee break. Don't go tell someone about the great appointment you just set up or the fantastic lead you got on a half-million-dollar listing.

Keep in mind that after you score an interview, there's no better time to score another one than right away. You don't want that lilt of enthusiasm to leave your voice. So start dialing.

On the other hand, if the call was a downer, don't let it get to you. Remind yourself that you don't need for everyone to say yes. You only need one or two or three or whatever you've set as your goal for that session.

Sometimes taking a deep breath helps clear your head and brush away unpleasant feelings. Then go for it.

Move through your farm directory systematically. Don't skip people because you don't like their names or you remember a previous unpleasant call. Stay positive, warm, and take each card in order. Do the best job you can, and you'll finish your last call that day with a sense of satisfaction.

That's the most anyone can ever ask of you. Do the best you can, the best way you know how, experiment on doing it better, and, most important of all, keep trying.

The world is full of quitters. It's the ones who don't give up who stand out.

Summary

Right down to the last click of the receiver, there's a right and wrong way to handle a call. For the wrap-up, the proper procedure is this:

1. Set up the appointment.
2. Repeat the time, place, and date.
3. Give the prospect your name and number.
4. Thank the prospect.
5. Be the last to hang up.

If the call ends without an appointment, be as courteous and kind as ever. Let the prospect know that you'll be calling back again — "just to see if things have changed."

Keep tabs on yourself by jotting down how you need to follow up the call right after it's over. You may want to set up a system so you know how to put the prospect in your next batch of farming calls. Or you may want to write a reminder to call back in a few days. Or you may want to send a special thank-you note. Whatever type of follow-up you choose, be prompt and be efficient.

Plunge right into your next call, without taking a break. Keep up the momentum and it'll work for you. Right after you've set up one interview, your enthusiasm gives you a great edge for setting up another.

Always remember to end every call on a warm and personal note, an echo of the way you started the call. Hold that note until the prospect's final click signals the call is over. Then start again.

14. When Your Phone Rings

When the phone rings, a top-notch real estate professional knows that a golden opportunity could lie on the other end.

Sadly, though, all too often the call is handled simply as a request for information. Sales techniques are ignored at exactly the time when they could do the most good, because when someone calls in, you know they're in the market. Don't let them get away.

Typically, the call is from someone who has spotted an ad in the paper or written down your number from a sign in front of a house. Either way, they've gone to some trouble to reach you.

When the call results from an ad, that tells you which ads are working. File the information away in your mental computer and pull it out later when you're doing the next set of ads. It's always good to know what type of copy or listing is triggering the most responses.

Now, even if someone has jotted down your name and number and taken the time to call, that doesn't mean they know what they want.

Maybe they liked the seclusion of the house. Or

the redwood trim. Or the shade trees in the front yard. Something struck them — if you find out what it was, you can suggest other homes they might want to see.

Frankly, hardly anyone ever buys the home they circle in the paper or see as they drive along the street. When they do buy, it's probably another home with the same feature that first nabbed their attention. Your job, from the moment you answer the phone, is the same as it is when you're making your farming calls: to get an appointment.

Turn a Caller into a Client

Whether you get an appointment from an inbound inquiry call depends a lot on your ability to turn a caller into a client. There are specific things you can do that will intensify the caller's interest and turn it into desire.

Remember, when people call in, the interest is already there. Assume they're ready to buy. Even if they say they're just looking, don't believe them. If they're interested enough to look, they can be interested enough to buy. In short, treat every call you receive as a hot prospect.

The Right Time to Answer

Believe it or not, there is a right time to answer the phone. No, it's not on the first ring. That would make you seem too anxious. It's not on the fifth ring, either. That's making someone wait too long. By then, they're thinking you're not on your toes.

The right time to answer is on the third or fourth ring.

Letting a phone ring twice gives you a few seconds to mentally separate from whatever you're doing. You can take a deep breath, pump up your enthusiasm and answer with an excited lilt in your voice.

The last thing in the world you want to do is to answer sounding rushed or impatient or in the middle of something else.

Every prospect deserves your full attention. Make sure you give it to them.

Take Charge

From the beginning of the call, take control. All too often real estate agents let the caller lead the way. That doesn't help them or you.

Statistics prove that most callers don't really know what they want in a home. They need someone to interpret what they want, show them what's available, and help them make a good decision.

Remember that real estate is a highly complicated field. Especially if you're not engrossed in it 40 or more hours a week. Things change quickly. Keeping up on the latest dips in the market, fluctuations in mortgage rates, special types of financing — that takes an expert — *you*.

When a caller is defensive and tries to take charge, often it's because other agents have led him down a garden path, refusing to give any information unless he meets with them.

Nothing will kill potential interest faster.

Whatever interest a client has, you need to nurture and encourage it.

Be Helpful

You can be helpful and, at the same time, let a caller know you could help even more if they'd be willing to let you do it.

But you have to persuade them that's true. One way is to have all the information they might need at your fingertips.

Whenever you work the floor, make sure you've seen the latest "sold" sheets. Know which properties have offers on them, which are in escrow, and which have closed. Then for every house your office lists, have in mind two or three alternative houses.

Maybe they're in the same type of neighborhood, are in the same price range, or offer some of the same features. Since most people don't buy the home they call about, always be ready to suggest others.

The Bare Bones of an Incoming Call

Just as we sketched out your farming calls step-by step, now we're going to give you a road map for calls you receive. Remember, you're the person in charge, even if you didn't initiate the call.

Introduction — Here you identify your company and politely ask how you can help the caller. You don't give your name.

Ask Qualifying Questions — Sometimes this is necessary, other times the caller offers it without your asking. Basically, all you're doing is finding out what he or she wants to know.

Give Requested Information — Here you fill in

the answers for the caller, giving him or her the satisfaction that you're not putting him or her off.

Ask Probing Questions — Sound familiar? Now you begin moving back into the framework of a farming call. By asking questions, you look for what the client really wants. You begin to cultivate your relationship with the prospect.

Give Alternatives — In some ways, this is a variation of a close. You meet the caller's request, but you're also ready with alternatives. This is where you begin suggesting them.

Overcome Objections — Since they haven't thought about it before (and since human nature is the way it is), they're bound to come up with objections. Handle them the same way you do the objections in farming calls. Be polite, warm, friendly, positive, and intelligent.

Close — Ideally, your close here is also the same as on a farming call, setting up an appointment. But if that's out of the question, go for dropping off some information at their house or sending them something in the mail — anything to keep the contact alive and give yourself a reason to build a relationship.

Wrap-Up — Once again, hopefully, you're confirming all the details of the appointment you've just arranged. Or at the least, you're writing down the caller's name and address. Remember to check everything twice. Stay as warm and courteous as ever. Thank them for their time. Reassure them they're taking the right step. And *always* let them hang up first.

Of course, that's all crystal clear to you and no more explanation is needed. But just in case, here's a sample script for an incoming call, with each section marked for easy reference.

What to Say When You Answer

Once you've done your homework, you're ready for the first call. It rings twice. On the third ring, you pick it up and say, "Jenkins Realty, good morning. How may I help you?"

See something missing in there? That's right — you don't give your name when you answer the phone.

If you do, they're sure to forget it. They have no idea who you are or what you're like. So your name is meaningless.

If you hold it back, you can toss it in later during the call. By then, they'll know a little bit about you, and chances are much better they'll remember it.

There's another plus, too. If you wait, when you do finally give your name, you can ask for theirs in return.

We all know how reluctant many callers are to identify themselves. Waiting until you've established some rapport is a good way to break down their resistance.

Ask Plenty of Questions

Earlier we talked about the similarities between calls you receive and calls you make. There's no reason why you shouldn't treat every call that comes into your office with the same care you give to your farming by phone.

Most of the tips work equally well for both types of calls. In fact, you should be able to steer an incoming call in exactly the same direction you steer your farming calls.

How? With questions.

Questions are the heartbeat of good prospecting calls, because they draw people out and begin to build a relationship.

You can do the same thing with incoming calls.

But a word of caution: Some overzealous agents try to move too quickly. If a caller asks a question, they feed another one back to him or her.

This technique works, but only if you also give the caller some information. If you play your cards too close to your chest, your prospect will feel terribly frustrated. He or she could easily wind up in an angry outburst and hang up the phone. It happens more times than you care to think.

Callers have lots of reasons why they may not want to meet with you right off the bat. Maybe they have another agent. Or they still just want to think about it. There are ways to handle all of their objections. Many of these methods will remind you of how we dealt with objections during prospecting calls. Here, too, the same rules of courtesy and kindness apply.

Finally, if the tables are turned and a caller asks you a question you can't answer right away, don't try to fudge it. Be honest. Admit you don't know, and promise that as soon as you hang up, you'll check it out and get right back to him or her. Then do it.

If you're honest and you keep your word, people will respect you for it.

How to Get a Caller's Name

Callers often don't like to give their names because they feel you'll start pressuring them. Or they may feel obligated to you.

Being anonymous does have its advantages. People can't call you back. You can ask whatever you like. When you hang up, that's it. The relationship is over. But for someone who's in the market for a home, not giving a name has definite drawbacks. It's up to you to point them out.

First, though, there are few things you can do to try to coax a caller into identifying himself.

When someone calls in, there's a good chance you'll have to put him or her on hold for a few seconds. Just so you can dig out the right property description.

When you get back on the line, you have a perfect opportunity to gently inquire, "Thank-you so much for waiting. May I ask who's calling, please?"

Depending on your tone of voice, this can come across as kind or as pushy. Of course, if the caller does give you his or her name, start using it right away and keep on using it throughout the conversation.

If you have difficulty getting the caller's name, be patient. Wait until you sense the person is totally at ease with you on the phone; then feel free to give your name and ask for his or hers.

Instead of a blunt "May I ask your name?" try the softer approach, "My name is Gina Jordan. And your name is . . . ?"

If you still have trouble getting the caller's name, you can always offer to drop more information by his or her house or put something in the mail right away. Then the caller will have to give you his or her name and address. But the caller won't feel you're being overly aggressive. Instead he or she will see how kind and helpful you are.

Here's a list of some of the material that might interest them:

* Map of the area they asked about
* Brochures about your company
* Pictures and descriptions of properties similar to the one they asked about
* Financing information
* Booklets on special services you offer

Of course, your first choice would be to drop information off at the caller's home. Since so many callers want simply to drive by properties, offering to hand-deliver materials in advance can be very helpful. That way, you're able to meet with the caller, but it's not as pressured a situation as showing a property.

However, if a face-to-face meeting is out of the question, settle for the next best thing — getting something in the mail. When you do this, as soon as you hang up, check the telephone directory for the caller's phone number. Make a note to call him or her back in two or three days. Then stuff the information in an envelope, with a note and your business card, and mail it as soon as you can.

When you call, the person may be surprised to hear your voice. But you can swoop right past the surprise and get to the heart of the matter by asking if he or she has seen the property and what he or she thinks of it. Don't give the prospect any time to wonder about how you got the phone number.

Every so often, you'll run into someone who has really been burned. Even if you directly ask for his or her name, he or she will refuse to give it. What can you do then?

Something like this might be in order: "I can appreciate your not wanting to give out your name. But every day new listings are coming into our office. And the best buys are snapped up right away. Some don't even last 24 hours."

Then stop. Let the caller respond. Don't push any more. You've made your point. If you use this approach and it works, it's very important that you make good your promise. Don't say you'll check listings every day for someone and then not do it. After a week or two without hearing from you, they'll move on to someone else. And they'll think you were lying just to get their name.

Even if there aren't any listings that meet their needs, call anyway. Let them know you're looking out for them.

Dealing with Specific Questions

When a prospect asks for specific details on a listing, what he or she really wants to know is something more. What does it mean if a living room is 12' by 13'? If the room is all glass, it will have a very different feeling than a paneled room with rustic beams across the ceiling.

Tell the prospect how the room feels, too. Keep in mind that we think in pictures. Use your words to create enticing images in the prospect's mind.

For example, if the prospect asks, "How big is the family room?" your response might go like this: "The family room is just the kind of place it's nice to curl up in during the winter. You can sit in front of an enormous fire, watch the afternoon sun filtering down through the trees outside, and see the birds in the backyard. It's a comfortable room, with one entire wall of brick and a floor-to-ceiling bookcase, big enough for books and knicknacks. On paper, the dimensions are 10' by 13'. But the large windows make it seem bigger."

Or they may ask, "How big is the lot?" Instead of giving them the dimensions straight up, you should respond something like, "The lot will surprise you. From the street, it doesn't seem very large. But the back is breathtaking. When you go out the door, you're on an old brick Spanish patio. Where it ends, the stucco terraces begin — yards and yards of them on a gently sloping lawn. In one garden, you can grow roses. In another, cactus. There's plenty of room. At night, you can sit outside and see all the city lights. It feels like another world."

The Price — To Tell or Not to Tell?

When you answer the phone and someone says, "I'm calling about a house I saw in the paper," or "I just drove by a house and saw your sign," you know there's one thing uppermost in their mind — price.

Some companies feel that giving out the price of a listing is fine. Others caution that it should be held back and that you should push instead to show the property.

When someone's asking about price, what they really want to know is if it's in their range. Looks can be deceiving.

Once I drove by a slightly run-down redwood cottage on a large lot. Calling the listing agent, I discovered that the price was more than $200,000.

I was shocked. It looked like a small older home. But there was a lot more there than I could see from the street. It turns out that it had four bedrooms and a pool.

If a particular property is clearly out of the

question for the caller, ask what price range he or she's in. Know the market well enough to have some other houses in mind. Don't write someone off just because the property the person is calling about is beyond his or her reach. It just shows the caller has good taste.

When a caller does ask about price and you give it to him or her, be sure to add on important elements. For example, is the owner willing to carry some of the financing? Has the price recently been reduced? Is there a low assumable mortgage? Include some of the specifics, because we all know that what a mortgage really boils down to is the monthly payment, not the asking price.

But gloss over the financing specifics quickly. Don't dwell on how much it's going to cost. Dwell instead on how wonderful the home is. If they talk price, you talk benefits. People buy things not because they can afford them, but because they want them.

Start stirring up an emotional interest in the home and you'll have a head start on getting an appointment.

Incoming Callers' Objections

When talking to a prospect who calls you, you'll hear certain objections more than others. But remember that for every objection, there's a positive response.

You may want to copy down some of the responses that follow and slip them into your script book. Put them in a special section for incoming calls. The better prepared you are, the more effectively you'll handle each and every call.

"I Just Want to Drive By"

One of the most common phrases you'll hear from callers is that they would simply like to drive by the property and then call you back if they're still interested. This situation is dangerous because a prospect looking on his or her own cannot be sold. A good response to the "drive by" request is this: "It is important to see a house from the outside. I'll be more than happy to drive you there. Then if you want to go inside, we can do it on the spot. But first, maybe I can save you some time. Tell me, how many children do you have?"

"Let Me Think It Over and I'll Call You Back"

"I'll think it over" is another crusher response from a prospect who needs to be converted into a client. Here a good response might be something like this: "I can understand that. You're making an important decision. Unfortunately, in the market today, there isn't a lot of time to decide. Good listings like this one disappear in a few days. You do think that timing is critical, don't you?"

Adding a sense of urgency is one of the most effective ways to deal with indecision.

"I Drove By and It Looks Very Run-down"

When the prospect is calling because of a "for sale" sign — and he or she has already seen the exterior of the house — you're liable to get much more specific objections, such as, "It looks so run-down."

Remember, of course, that it can't be that bad in

the prospect's mind since he or she did take the time to call you.

Nonetheless, you need to respond to the specific objection with a very specific response. To a "rundown" objection, you may respond with, "Yes, but look at its price. You can't touch other four-bedroom homes in Diamond Bar for under $150,000. You don't want to miss this opportunity."

Sample Incoming Call

It's Sunday afternoon and Agent Wilma Wilcox is working the floor. In front of her is the Sunday paper, with her office's listings circled. Also nearby is a sheet on which she has grouped similar houses by neighborhood, price, or features. For every listing, she has two or three alternatives. The Multiple Listing Book is open and waiting. Her Incoming Call Forms are ready. The phone rings.

Introduction

Agent: Homebound Real Estate. May I help you?

Prospect: Yes. I'm calling about a home I saw advertised in today's paper.

Ask Qualifying Questions

Agent: Could you please tell me what the ad said?

Prospect: It says it's a four-bedroom ranch on a half acre in Mundelein.

Agent: Oh, yes. We've had quite a few calls on that home today. A lot of people are interested. It's a beautiful property — the home is charming and there's plenty of land. Let me get the specifics for you. Just a minute, please.

(Pause for brief hold)

Give Requested Information

Agent: Thank-you for waiting. The home is listed for $175,000. It's 3,000 square feet, with a kitchen the whole family can eat in, a dining room that's perfect for entertaining, four good-sized bedrooms with closets big enough for clothes and toys, three baths, and from every room you can look through wide windows to the rolling countryside. The workmanship is of a quality you don't find very often anymore. And best of all, there's a wonderful sense of serenity in the home. Tell me, how many are there in your family?

Ask Probing Questions

Prospect: Three children, my wife, and myself.

Agent: Do you own your home now?

Prospect: No, we just moved to this area about a year ago. I wanted to rent for awhile first, so we'd have a better idea of where we wanted to live.

Agent: That was a wise decision. Then you've been out to Mundelein and you like it?

Prospect: Yes, I like the country feeling, even though it's close to the city. But I'm not sure I want to pay more than $150,000.

Trial Close 1

Agent: We have a number of listings in Mundelein. I can think of two or three that might interest you. I'd be

247

happy to drive you out there this afternoon. Either five or six o'clock is fine for me. What's best for you?

Prospect: I appreciate the offer, but I'd rather just drive out there myself. Then if I'm interested, I'll call you back.

Overcome Objections

Agent: I can certainly understand your wanting to see the homes first. But sometimes it's hard to tell what a home is really like if you only see it from the street.

Prospect: That's true. But I really would rather do it this way.

Trial Close 2

Agent: Whatever you like. However, I would appreciate it if you'd let me send you some information on the homes we have in that area.

Prospect: Sure. That's fine.

Wrap-Up

Agent: And your name is?

Prospect: Tom. Tom Pitzer.

Agent: Is that spelled P-I-T-Z-E-R?

Prospect: That's correct.

Agent: And your address, Mr. Pitzer?

Prospect: 11273 East Bay Road, Chesterton, Indiana 46304.

Agent: 11273 East Bay Road, Chesterton, Indiana 46304. Great. I'll have the information on its way to you this afternoon. Now, if you want to drive by the properties before you receive it, let me give you the addresses. They are: 700 Lincoln Street, 809 Grant Street, and the property you called about is at 912 Johnson Street. Do you have a map of the Mundelein area?"

Prospect: Yes, I do.

Agent: Good. You won't have any trouble finding the homes. Just take the first DeKalb exit off the freeway. Then turn right at the first stoplight. They're all in the Terrace Acres subdivision.

If you have any more questions, Mr. Pitzer, my name is Wilma Wilcox and I'll be more than happy to help you. The number here, again, is 861-2345.

Prospect: Well, Wilma, thank-you. It's been a real pleasure to deal with someone so helpful.

Agent: Thank-you, Mr. Pitzer. And I hope you see something you like.

Prospect: Good-bye.

Agent: Good-bye.

Prospect: CLICK (prospect hangs up first).

Agent: CLICK (Wilma hangs up last).

Wilma then goes straight to the phone book, looks up the Pitzers' phone number and makes a note to call them Wednesday evening. Then she puts together the information he wanted and, on her way home, drops it off at the post office.

Switching from Information to Conversation

During this conversation, Wilma gave the caller everything he asked for. Then she quickly moved into a few questions of her own. Within a minute, the call moved from strictly professional grounds to a more personal and warmer note. There was give and take. In other words, a real conversation developed.

Knowing the right moment to switch from an information call to a conversation can be tricky. But here are a few ways to try it:

Prospect: Well, I like that house. But it's out of my price range.

Agent: There are three other homes in the same neighborhood that might meet your needs. But before I tell you about them, would you mind telling me how many there are in your family?

Prospect: I'm calling about that cute country cottage you're advertising in today's paper. The one for $80,000.

Agent: Oh, that's a charming home. Lots of character. Tell me, what size home are you looking for?

Prospect: I'd like to know more about the three-bedroom, two-bath home that just went on the market.

Agent: You must mean the house on Elm Street. Is that it?

Prospect: Yes.

Agent: I'm sorry, but the owners just accepted an offer. How long have you been looking for a new home?

Prospect: I'm calling about the "unique contemporary" advertised in yesterday's paper. Can you tell me where it is?

Agent: I'd be happy to. It's in the Canyon Park area. Are you familiar with the neighborhood?

Prospect: I'd like more information on the older home you're advertising, the one with hardwood floors and a fireplace.

Agent: Why, certainly. I'll be glad to help to you. The home is a well-designed colonial, in excellent shape, located in the Bradley School District. Where do you live?

If you lead into a conversation near the beginning of a call, don't keep running on with a series of questions. Switch back and forth from asking questions to giving information about the property. That way, the prospect will be satisfied that you're answering the questions. And you'll have the satisfaction of finding out what you need to know.

See how easy it is to lead into questions? You just have to use your intuition to know the right moment to begin.

If you start too early in the call and you sense the prospect tightening up, go back to giving information. Then try again in half a minute.

Turning Renters into Buyers

By now, you should have a handle on how to transform a negative into a positive. But there's one other important area to discuss before we move on. That's how to turn a renter into a buyer.

251

Everyone you know who rents is a potential client. In time, if you keep up the relationship, they will be clients. After all, who wants to be giving money to the government if they don't have to? And why should they be lining the landlord's pockets when they could be filling their own?

For anyone paying rent, owning a home is worth considering. For personal reasons, some may prefer to keep renting. But down the road, almost all of them will be looking to buy.

A number of states offer special financing to first-time home buyers. That's something you should know about. It could make a big difference when you're outlining the wonderful advantages of ownership.

The potential market among renters is so great, some agents manage to convert four out of every five calls for rental properties into buyers. That's right. Four out of every five. Know your tax laws. Find out about special programs for new home buyers. Then you can be among the top converters, too.

To give you some ideas on how to handle calls about rental properties, here's a sample script:

Agent: Good morning, Turner Realty. May I help you?

Prospect: Yes. We're looking for a three-bedroom house to rent. Do you have anything available?

Agent: I wish I could say yes. Maybe I can help you anyway. How much rent did you want to pay?

Prospect: About $800 a month.

Agent: Well, that's reasonable. How many are there in your family?

Prospect: My husband and I have two children.

Agent: In addition to the three bedrooms, were you looking for anything special in a home? Perhaps a big yard or a family room?

Prospect: I'd love a fenced yard so the children would have a safe place to play. My husband says he wants a garage; but if I had to, I could talk him out of it. As for a family room, that would be nice. But a big living room is just as good.

Agent: There is a three-bedroom home that seems to fit your requirements. It's in an excellent neighborhood. The backyard is totally fenced in. And with a small down payment, the home could be yours for about $900 a month. When you figure in all the money you save on taxes, that's actually less than you'd be paying in rent. I could show you the home this afternoon. Is four o'clock all right, or would you prefer six o'clock?

Prospect: Well, we really weren't interested in buying.

Agent: I can understand that. Owning a home is a big commitment. But if you're willing to pay $800 a month in rent, it's something you should consider. By owning a home, you'd save thousands of dollars every year. May I ask if you've ever owned a home?

Prospect: No, we've been moving around too much.

Agent: What if I show you the house we were talking about? It's vacant, so we won't be disturbing anyone. Then we can sit down and talk about ways you might be able to swing it. Is tonight convenient for you, or would you prefer tomorrow morning?

Prospect: Ummm, tonight's okay. If we make it six o'clock, then my husband can join us.

Agent: Wonderful. My name is Roberta Robinson. And yours is . . ?

Prospect: Carolyn Davidson.

Agent: Nice to meet you, Mrs. Davidson. Now where shall I pick you up?

Prospect: We live at 313 N. Elm Street here in town.

Agent: 313 N. Elm Street. Great. I'll be there at six o'clock. I look forward to seeing you.

Prospect: Thank-you. See you soon. Good-bye.

Agent: Good-bye, Mrs. Davidson.

Prospect: CLICK (prospect hangs up first).

Agent: CLICK (agent hangs up last).

Leaving Messages

On this subject, you'll find recommendations on both sides of the fence. Some people say it's okay to leave messages on sales calls. Others suggest calling back later so you can talk with the prospect directly. If you want to leave a message, make it assertive and positive.

For example, if you're calling the neighbors of a home you just listed, your message might go something like this: "This is Jeffrey Donaldson, with Thompson Realty. I'm helping Ken Simmons down the block find a buyer for his home and I wanted to talk to you about it. My number is 861-6587. That's 861-6587. I'd appreciate it if you would call me back sometime this afternoon. Thank-you."

If you can, throw in a little teaser. Make the person wonder, What do they want to talk to me about? You don't want them thinking, Oh, all he wants to do is list my home, too. Then they'll never call you back.

Superaggressive real estate professionals tend to leave messages like, "It's critical that Mr. Gephart call me back immediately."

My advice? Avoid that style. If they do call you back, they're in for a big letdown when it turns out that what you want is relatively minor. Before your relationship begins, you've destroyed the potential for trust.

Look how much better it is to say something like this: "Mention to Mr. Gephart that if it's at all possible, we'd really like to talk to him today."

If he doesn't call back, call again. If he's still not available, check for the best time to try again. Most people in this kind of situation are really helpful. They're usually embarrassed, too.

If a child answers the phone or someone who you don't feel will get the message straight, don't try leaving just a name and number. If they don't know you, that's a little cold. Instead ask what time the person you want to talk to will be home.

If the prospect has an answering machine, try one of the preceding teaser messages — with a mild sense of urgency. You can be almost positive he or she will get the message, along with the added benefit of hearing how warm and pleasant your voice is. If the prospect doesn't return the message, keep trying. You'll find him or her home eventually.

If you do run into someone who's hard to catch at home, calling around 9 a.m. is a good idea. Especially on Saturdays. Hardly anyone stirs outside of their yard before 10 a.m. on Saturday.

Taking Notes

One of the key advantages of working over the phone is the wonderful ability you have to take notes. In face-to-face meetings, you don't want to disrupt eye contact — jotting down every word someone is saying is enough to make anyone nervous. But over the phone, they'll never even know.

For note taking to be effective, you need to develop a system where you're focusing not on what you're writing, but on what the person is saying. Shorthand, of course, is the perfect solution. But few of us are going to take the time to learn it. So we all have to come up with our personal scribbling systems.

In Chapter 5, I presented a Buyer File Form which you'll want to keep handy while working the floor. Chances are that you'll be able to fill in the date and ad called about right off the top. The name and address will probably have to wait until later in the call.

If you're fortunate enough to run into a real conversationalist, the back side of the card is great for additional notes.

Also on the back keep your list of contacts. If you've set up an interview during your first conversation, write down the date, time, and place. That way you'll be able to keep track of when and how often you're touching base.

Initially don't worry about taking too many notes. Instead worry about taking too few. Within a few weeks, you'll be able to pare down your note taking so it won't seem as cumbersome.

Remember to write down the name as soon as the person gives it to you. Keep referring to it throughout the call. It's especially good to use the name just before making a point that deserves special emphasis. That way, the prospect will be paying more attention.

When working on the phone, it's also a good idea to keep nearby several different colored pencils or pens. Take down your basic information in regular pencil. Then use the colored pens to highlight anything you want to think about or follow up later.

Taking Messages

Trying to find people who can take good messages is a problem that plagues almost every office in this country. That's especially true for real estate agents, where often you don't have a receptionist.

Here's a simple rule: If you want people to take good messages for you, take good messages for them.

Some experts recommend that you write down all kinds of extraneous facts. But when it gets right down to it, all you need to know is the time the person called, his or her name, and telephone number. You're not going to want someone else in your office handling your clients for you. So detailed messages are *not* usually necessary.

But even getting the name and number straight can be a problem for some people. It helps to have message forms. Trying to locate a scrap of paper on a desk piled high with work is like looking for a needle in a haystack. But a bright pink message form really stands out.

When you're taking a message for someone else, don't forget to double-check the caller's name and number. If you have questions about the spelling, ask.

Often in real estate, friends tell other friends about us and gives them our numbers. If they call and the message-taker transposes two digits, forget it. They'll think we just didn't bother to call back. And we'll have no idea how to find the right number. That's why taking good messages in a real estate office is so important.

If you want to see how your messages are handled when you're out of the office, call yourself. See if the person answering is courteous and warm, if he or she repeats the number and name to verify them. If he or she doesn't, mention it when you're back in the office.

Taking good messages is something most of us never bother to think about — not until someone brings it to our attention.

If you're on the floor and someone calls for an agent who's with a client, generally the best thing to do is take a message. Then, as soon as the agent is free, he or she can return the call.

That avoids using the hold button, or making the caller feel unimportant when you return and say, "I'm sorry, he's with someone else right now." It's better to be up front about it from the beginning.

A final but crucial point: If your handwriting is hard to read, take the time to print phone messages. It will save you tons of aggravation and ill feelings from other agents in your office.

Answering Machines

Some agents use answering machines at home, others don't. Some offices have them on when everyone leaves for the day; others don't.

Before I got a machine of my own, I hated them. I found them to be impersonal, mechanical, and ugly. But for business reasons, I had no choice. Now every time I leave the house, even just to sit outside, the machine is on. It's a wonderful convenience, although the idea of being on call 24 hours a day still bothers me. Frankly, I don't know how agents live without them.

Buying a machine can cost you anywhere from $50 to $300, depending on the number of bells and whistles you want. On almost every model, you can select how many rings you want before the machine picks up the call. Since only a few offer three rings, go with four.

It's best to have a machine that lets your messages go as long as the caller wants. My first answering machine wound up cutting off about one out of every five calls, and people got very annoyed.

Usually your greeting is limited to about 20 seconds, after which the machine automatically puts on a tone. Then the caller knows to begin the message.

Almost essential these days is remote control. When you're calling in for your messages, as the greeting plays, you signal the machine with a special code (generally one of the buttons on a touch-tone phone), identifying you as the owner.

After the machine plays back the messages, you again hit the buttons for another signal and the machine sets itself up for more calls.

As far as choosing a phone answering machine, it's really up to you. My experience has shown, however, that you get what you pay for with them. And since they may mean the difference between getting a message or not, you might as well get a good one. On the other hand, many agents pour out a lot of money for features they'll never use.

Summary

After pages and pages of talking about calls you make, we finally got around to calls you receive. What we found is that they're not much different than the calls you make. Some of the beginning steps vary, but within a few minutes, you should be working on turning that caller into a client.

People call in because they've spotted a classified ad or driven by a house with your sign out front. Fewer than 10% of the people will actually buy the property they call about. That's why it's a good idea to have in mind two or three alternatives for every listing. If they're interested in one, why not another?

Basically, the rundown for an incoming call goes like this:

1. *Introduction* — Identify the company. Ask if you can help. Never give your name.
2. *Ask Qualifying Questions* — What does the caller want to know?
3. *Give Information* — Satisfy his or her curiosity.
4. *Ask Probing Questions* — Ask a few things yourself. Begin building a relationship.
5. *Suggest Alternatives* — Isn't there another house they might be interested in?
6. *Overcome Objections* — Once again. (Can't anyone ever agree the first time?)
7. *Close* — If the prospect doesn't want an appointment, ask if you can drop off some materials at their house or send them in the mail.
8. *Wrap-Up* — Courteously confirm whatever you've arranged, thank them, and be the last to hang up.

One fertile field worth exploring is renters. Some skillful agents convert into home buyers up to four out of every five callers looking for rental property. When it makes such good financial sense to buy, you've got a lot going for you.

What's one of the biggest advantages of working over the phone? You can take all the notes you want and no one sees you doing it. In the beginning, err on the side of taking excess notes. Better to know too much than too little.

As for leaving messages (if you do), make them clever ones. Gently tease someone into calling you back, but never mislead them. And avoid the dramatics.

If you take messages for others, take good ones. Then you can expect them to return the favor.

Finally, get ahold of the agent's best friend: Give in and buy an answering machine. That way you'll never come home again wondering how many people have been trying to reach you. You could be amazed at how popular you are!

15. Keeping in Touch by Phone

There's probably no better way to keep in touch with your prospects and clients than by telephone. In about 10 seconds, you can dial a number. In another two or three seconds, they'll be on the line. Then you can take as much or as little time as you need. It's a wonderfully flexible instrument, suitable for all kinds of purposes. Sometimes that simply means saying, "I'm here if you ever need me."

Making a Commitment to Your Clients

Never forget a client and never let a client forget you. Let that be your secret to success.

Sales experts say that getting one new client costs 20 times more than holding on to an old one. The people you've helped already trust you. They know you'll do a good job; and they like you. You can concentrate on how to do what's best for them.

But that doesn't work if you close a sale and forget your client. When you call a year later, they'll know that times are slow and you're just shuffling through old client cards.

Once you've got a client, keep him or her — by keeping up the relationship. Maintaining contact should start right from the beginning. A client should never have to call you to find out what's happening.

Working with Sellers

If you represent a seller, keep him or her abreast of all the details. Let him or her know when an appraisal is scheduled, or when a photographer will be there, or when the house will appear in the Multiple Listing Book. Do him or her the courtesy of double-checking the wording for classified ads. Pass on the comments of prospective buyers. Make a point of calling at least once a week.

If there's a problem, don't hesitate to let your clients know. They can probably help you work it out.

It's up to you to keep the sellers aware of all of the work you're doing to earn that nice, juicy commission. To them, the sum probably seems exorbitant. If so, that's your fault. They don't realize all that you're doing for them. And they never will, unless you tell them — not directly, of course. Tell them subtly, by keeping them informed of every step in the process.

Working with Buyers

When you're representing buyers, stick to the once-a-week rule, too. Make a point of calling them.

Realize that finding a home is one of the things uppermost in your clients' minds. They're probably thinking about it several dozen times a day. Maybe they have a new thought about what to look for.

Maybe they'd like to try a different neighborhood. Be there when they need you.

You should call every buyer as soon as the new listings come out. If there's something they might like, schedule a showing right away. If nothing seems right for them, call them anyway. Let them know you're on your toes.

Calls like this are good for discussing a buyer's options. Many people don't realize that they can get a lot more house for their money if they're willing to have a rental unit in back. Or you could raise the question of whether they'd like a lease-option. Or maybe they'd also like to look at lots. The possibilities are endless. Make your clients aware of them.

Making Yourself Available

For buyers or sellers, do this: Tell them to feel free to call you if they ever need anything. Give them your home and work numbers. Explain that if you're not home, the answering machine will take their messages and you'll get back to them as soon as you can. This is an offer not many people make. But it can do wonders for cementing relationships.

Many of this country's wealthiest men and women make their mark not by grabbing for the almighty dollar, but by showing their passion for what they do. Wealth is almost secondary. Learn from their example. Put people and their needs first. Then you'll find your own needs will be met, too.

Through simple gestures, you can show your clients that they're important to you. Things like returning their calls promptly. Or leaving word when you leave the office as to what time you'll be back.

Another way is through making it easy for clients

to reach you. That means being sure you have enough telephone lines in the office so no caller ever gets a busy signal. It also means having conveniences like a "hold" button (so callers don't have to listen to the hustle and bustle of the office while they're waiting for you).

With all the options you have at your fingertips (such as call forwarding or call waiting), there's no longer any excuse for not answering promptly.

If you treat your clients well, your farm directory will start growing almost on its own. People will begin sending you their friends, relatives and neighbors. They'll talk about you at work, and maybe at their clubs and parties.

And remember, you have a much greater chance of closing a sale from a referral than from a cold farming call.

Don't think of a sale as the end of your relationship with a client. Think of it as the beginning of a new stage — where there's more opportunity to get to know each other.

Thank-You Calls

Thank-you calls can go a long way toward building a long-standing relationship — a key ingredient to successful farming. In addition, they also are useful in a different way.

We all know about "buyer's remorse." Especially when there's a handsome, expensive home involved. It's only natural that two or three weeks after moving in, your client will begin to have second thoughts.

That's the time to call. Just a friendly conversation and maybe a visit. You could congratulate your client on the wisdom of selecting that property. Maybe you could stroll through the neighborhood and point out the homes of prominent neighbors. Check to see if your client has any questions. Find out if everything's working out the way he or she expected.

Agents often forget the fact that they may know more about a neighborhood than the people who live there. People are always curious about where they live and who their neighbors are. On a follow-up visit, this is the perfect opportunity to talk about it. Reassure people that they've done the right thing. Make them feel good about their new home. Even if they have a few doubts, they're still excited about it.

Six-Month Checkup

If you don't want to call out of the blue every year or so, how often should you call a client?

About every six months. That's enough time so you won't become a pest, but it won't seem like the calls are an afterthought either.

The calls don't have to be long. Just long enough so you can make sure everything is okay at the house. If it isn't, maybe you can suggest a handyman or contractor or plumber they can call. If they've just added on or remodeled, why not drop by? See if they'd like to know how much more their house is worth.

If they're in an affluent area, after six months you may want to suggest they consider buying commercial or rental properties as an investment. When you ask, be sure to have a few in mind.

Or maybe they know someone else who's in the market to buy or sell their home. Someone they might never have suggested if you didn't bring it up.

Here's a short checklist for checking up:

- Are they still happy in the home?
- Is everything working all right?

- Anything new in the family?
- Would they be interested in any commercial or rental properties?
- Do they know anyone else who's thinking of buying or selling their home?

By keeping a conversation flowing naturally, your checkup calls won't seem forced or contrived. Ask about the family and how everyone is doing (you should have notes to coach you). Show a genuine concern for them and their home. Ask about how work is going. Maybe a job transfer is coming up. If you've really gotten to know your clients the way you should, you won't have to worry about running out of things to say.

About four years down the road, start dropping hints about the availability of some newer or bigger houses in the neighborhood. If there's a spark of interest, turn it into a fire. If the embers are cool, leave it be. They'll want to move eventually and you'll be there when they do.

Follow-Up Pays Off

The greatest downfall of most real estate professionals is their failure to follow up — close the deal, write the check, and they're off to another client. But the most successful agents don't work that way. They can't. Because they know that past clients are their bread and butter.

When you represent people in finding or selling a home, you learn things about them. You meet their family. You see how they live. You discover what little things they like to have around them.

Maybe someone is a bird lover who wants a lot of trees in the backyard. Or maybe the client is a computer expert who needs enough space for a home office. Or maybe they want a large family in a few years, so they buy a four-bedroom home.

For each one of your clients, you should know enough to be on the lookout for items of special interest. If you run across an article about stamp collecting and you have a client whose passion is stamps, slip the article into the mail, with a brief note and your card. Even if he or she has already seen the article, he or she will appreciate the thought.

You can do the same for a sports fan, a business-person, a mother, a fashion designer. We all have our own special interests.

The same goes for news in the local paper. If there's a wedding in the family, send a card. If there's a new baby, send another card. If there's a death, send your condolences.

Of course, it goes without saying that you should make a point of finding out your clients' birthdays and send special cards. Christmas cards are a must. Thanksgiving, Easter, and St. Patrick's Day cards are optional.

Just stay in touch on a warm and personal basis. One day, you'll be surprised at how many friends you've made over the years. And they really will be your friends, too.

Cellular Phones

Ten years ago, you'd never read a chapter like this in a book. But times change faster than we do. And there's something new that could belong in your car or briefcase.

What is it? A telephone. Cellular car phones are hot. Especially here in major metropolitan areas. Usually they're in upscale cars, but more and more, you see them in midsize cars, too.

When cellular phones first hit the market in 1982, they cost between $2,000 and $3,000. Outside of the cost, one of the biggest problems was the fact that few cities had a cellular radio network in place. Today, about 100 cities are equipped to handle car phoning — that's up from 73 cities just a year ago.

Here's how a cellular car phone works. When you press a button on the receiver, you plug into a radio network built just to transmit calls. In fact, your city is honeycombed with small transmitters for this system. No wires. No fuss.

Anyway, when you hit the button, you're on a radio channel. All you have to do is dial the phone number, just like an ordinary call. Once you're hooked into the radio channel, your call is transferred to regular local and long-distance phone networks. You can call anywhere in the world.

Prices for cellular phones aren't cheap. They generally run about $1,000 to $1,200, including installation. You can rent cellular phones, but the charges are again high.

The greatest expense is in the billing for the calls. You're billed for every second of radio time you use. And it doesn't matter if you placed the call or if someone called you. Some companies even charge for busy signals.

In the next decade, cellular phones will change the way we do business. From the answering machine, we've now moved another step closer to being continually on call.

If you do a lot of driving and live in an area "wired for cellular," you may want to consider the convenience of a cellular phone.

The bottom line is that car phones are another way to be there for your clients. And if you're there for them, they'll be there for you, too.

Summary

Like an old record, we keep playing the same song: Take care of your clients, and they'll take care of you, too.

Taking care of a client means keeping up the relationship. Don't close the deal and cut off the client. Stay in touch.

Keeping in touch starts right from the beginning of your relationship. No client should ever have to wonder what you're doing for them. It's your job to let them know. That means calling at least once a week. And it doesn't matter if it's a buyer or a seller. Otherwise, how will they ever know how hard you're working for them?

When a sale goes through, take the first step toward keeping up the contact with a thank-you call. If you call two or three weeks after the sale is final, you could head off a bad case of "buyer's remorse." When people buy something as expensive as a house, they need reassurance that they've done the right thing. It's just part of your job.

Then, in six months, start phoning on a regular basis. Don't make a pest out of yourself. Twice a year is fine. Just see how things are going or if there's anything new in the family. Maybe they'd be interested in investing in some property. Or do they know someone who's thinking of buying or selling their home?

In addition to your calls, send cards. Always send them at Christmas. But if you spot a wedding announcement or death notice or some other news about their family, let them know you're thinking of them with a card.

If you happen to come across an article a client might be interested in, pass it along. He or she will appreciate the thought.

The bottom line is: Be there for your clients. Make them feel free to call you at home or at work anytime they need to. Not many will take you up on the offer, but you'll create a lot of goodwill.

If you're out of the office a lot, consider a car phone. It's another way to stay in touch with the clients who give you and your family a living.

16. You Can Do It!

Now we're down to where the rubber meets the road. All the prep time in the world — the studying, the scriptwriting, the planning — is only an aid for making you more effective. Deciding to succeed — making that commitment — is entirely up to you.

Often it's the intangible aspects of our personality that determine whether we make a failure or success out of life. However, they're not absolutes.

We can change the way we are. With a little work, we can become more disciplined, more assertive, and more compassionate. If our will is strong enough, we can move mountains.

Will is something that books can't give you. Neither can hours of hard work. Or afternoons of role-playing. These kinds of things can help. But the depth of your commitment is measured by a choice you make with your mind, and then plant in your heart.

Strength of will can make a person great. It gives you the ability to come through, long after others have dropped away.

Law of Averages

Depending on your point of view, the law of averages in farming can work for you or against you.

Taking the negative approach, out of every 10 calls you make, you can expect 9 rejections. That can be hard to handle.

But if you're aware of the odds going in — if you're prepared to field any and all objections that you hear — go for it. Don't let fear of rejection stand in your way.

You can also take comfort in the fact that if you make enough calls, you're sure to strike the jackpot. You have to. The laws of mathematics say so. But at the first trace of discouragement, you can't stop. If you give in then, it's hopeless. Put aside your discouragement and know that the numbers are working for you.

Expect to succeed and you will.

How You Feel About Yourself Makes a Difference

Obviously we can't control every circumstance in our life. But each of us has the power to decide how we're going to respond to our circumstances.

For example, if you lose a job you can view the loss as simply freeing you for a better opportunity. Or you can take all the blame on your own little shoulders and tell yourself you're no good for anything.

In real estate, every day people will be accepting you or rejecting you. If you allow their momentary whims to control your self-image, you'll be on an emotional roller coaster the rest of your life. Your strength, your confidence, has to come from within.

That's something no one else can give you.

One of the best ways to develop a strong, secure inner confidence is by concentrating on what you want to *be* — not on what you want to *have*.

If you want certain character traits, you have a good chance of succeeding. Those are things you can control. And you can choose traits that almost guarantee success — things like honesty, self-discipline, hard work, and kindness.

But if you only go after the commission, you've lost out on a lot — not only financially, but personally as well.

Another important factor is that you should like what you do. When you talk real estate, your voice should light up with enthusiasm and interest. You should have a passion for your work and for the people you help.

Like what you do and be relaxed about it. Set realistic goals for yourself and keep revising them upward. But don't give yourself goals you can't achieve. Know your limitations, especially at the beginning of your farming efforts. Make allowances for them.

It also helps to cultivate a certain sense of indifference. One day you might be in the pits. The next day you might be on top of the world. Level yourself out. During the slump, know that a good time is just around the corner. During the good times, prepare for a month when business slackens.

Take each day as it comes. Be grateful for what it gives you. When obstacles come your way, look at them as challenges or learning opportunities. Don't let them pull you down.

Almost all of us want to succeed at what we do. We're willing to work long and hard to give it all we've got. But then we run into something like rejection.

Fear of failing or fear of rejection holds back more people than you'd ever guess. But anyone can overcome those fears if they're willing to face them and conquer them.

There are no pat answers on how to do that. For each of us, the opportunities come in different shapes and sizes. But one way to start is by making a commitment to work your farm with all the energy and enthusiasm you can. Then, when you run into a string of "no's," tell yourself you won't let them defeat you. Keep going until you've met your goal.

By taking control of your own life, you can be the person you want to be. And when you are, you'll find you already have the things you want and need.

Keep a Positive Outlook

Face it. Real estate is one of the most competitive games in town. If you can't discount your prices, what do you have to offer that's unique?

For starters — you. What you're selling isn't only a house or a service, it's you — the *you* that comes across in every letter, on every phone call, and in every personal visit.

You are different from any other agent in town and that can be a tremendous asset.

If people are going to trust you to help them make the biggest financial decision of their lives, they've got to like you. So do your best to have a winning personality.

Many years ago, Norman Vincent Peale handed out a few tips in his book, *The Power of Positive Thinking* (Prentice Hall, 1952).

Here's my own updated version:

1. Remember people's names. Using a name is a sign that an individual is important to you.

2. Make it easy for people to be with you. Be a comfortable person who puts others at ease.

3. Have a relaxed attitude toward life, taking the hard knocks in stride.

4. Make yourself an interesting person to talk to. Read the latest magazines, keep up with the local news, and know a little about a lot of things.

5. Encourage others. Be a positive and uplifting force in others' lives. Weed the "little negatives" out of your thinking and your speech.

6. Keep your focus on others, not on yourself. Don't spend all your time trying to impress people with how great you are. Instead be naturally humble.

7. Clear your mind of anger, jealousy, and envy. When misunderstandings happen, straighten them out right away. Don't harbor negative emotions.

8. If there's a rough edge to your personality, smooth it over.

9. Genuinely like every person you meet. If you do, they can't help liking you back.

Don't Sell — Help People Buy

It's an old, old saying, but never *sell* real estate. Always *help* your clients *buy* it. This means keeping a prospect's interest by putting your offer and your suggestions in terms that revolve around him or her. Don't think about what *you* want. The fact that you want a sale isn't going to make anybody buy from you. Think instead about what the other person wants.

Show how you can meet his or her personal needs. Maybe it's with a fast escrow. Or personal attention. Or walking through some papers. Whatever it is, make your offer desirable from the prospect's point of view.

During your call, remember to focus not on what you can't do, but on what you can do. A prospect might ask, "Could you also handle the escrow?" You can respond, "What I can do is work closely with the escrow company, calling every day and keeping track of every piece of paper. Believe me, I would never just turn over the paperwork to a company without following through as closely as I can. I know how important it is for you to be in a new home as soon as possible."

This example brings up a key point. Part of your job involves making a prospect feel you understand him or her. That's crucial to your relationship.

I remember visiting scores of agents when looking for a home. They kept showing me pictures of tract houses, the last thing in the world I wanted. They didn't hear me. They didn't understand me.

If you want to find the right house for the right person, work at understanding him or her. Pick up on the little idiosyncrasies of your prospect's personality. Don't think that what's important to you is also important to him or her. We're all different.

Sometimes, even when clients have some doubts, they'll go ahead with buying a home because you're so sure it's the right thing to do. And you understand their needs so well.

It is hard for some people to make decisions. At times, we have to help them along. But we should only do it when we're persuaded that it's what they really want and need.

It helps to use words like "we" instead of "I." And to talk in the present tense instead of the past. Make people feel involved and important. Give them the attention we all hunger for.

And remember, people don't like to buy or pay or sell. They like to *own*.

Nine Ways to Kill a Farm Call

Just as a refresher, let's go over some of the absolute no-no's for your farming calls. Remember your calls are supposed to be warm and personal, built around developing a relationship between you and your prospect. Nothing will kill a budding relationship faster than if you do any of the following:

1. Interrupt a prospect or finish his or her sentences.
2. Try to educate your prospect.
3. Force your own feelings, prejudices, and opinions onto your prospect.
4. Miss the feelings behind a prospect's words.
5. Misinterpret what a prospect is saying.
6. Overly flatter a prospect.
7. Sound rushed or impatient.
8. Have a complicated offer, making it hard for the prospect to understand.
9. Lie or exaggerate.

How to Become a Farming Superstar

So you've resolved to farm your field diligently. You've got the system set up. The first calls have been better than you expected. You're gung ho for three months, but then you hit a slump. What happened?

In this business, there are ups and downs. But there's also the personal factor. Often someone who's polishing up his or her skills follows through for awhile, but then he or she gets tired of it. The person hits a hump he or she can't seem to get over.

This is where your true colors are revealed. Here the top-notch professionals will dig in their heels, grit their teeth, and declare, "Nothing is going to stop me. I'm going to make a success of this if it's the last thing I do!"

Less-determined agents will blame the slump on a lack of leads or a slow season or financial conditions. They'd never dream of pinning the blame right where it belongs — on themselves.

Everyone has slow times. When you fall into one, check your attitude. Are you still as enthusiastic as ever? Does conviction still radiate in every word of your farming calls? Or has a note of boredom set in? Are you getting tired of the uphill struggle?

If you are, pull yourself out of it. Remember the vigor with which you first attacked farming. Recapture it.

At times like these, often the hardest part is admitting to ourselves that we're the ones with the problem, not our uninterested prospects.

If we're not enthusiastic about what we're doing, how can we possibly expect them to be? So stay out of a slump by watching your own attitude. Guard and nurture your enthusiasm. If you see it slipping away, do something to pump it back up.

You know, there is a smart way to approach farming — a way that will save you time, money, and grief. It involves keeping records and evaluating yourself on a regular basis.

After a few months, when you see where you're most effective, channel your energies into that area. Build on what you're best at. Put all of these principles to work in a personal way. Find out what brings in the best results for you. But do it intelligently. Don't just cut out the things you don't like to do. Recognize that there are certain basics that are essential to success.

Ask yourself these questions:

1. Am I familiar with every listing my office is handling? Do I know which listings are similar?

2. Do I check new listings as soon as they come out every week?

3. Do I make a point of driving through my farm once a week?

4. Do I have a set schedule every month for farming calls?

5. Do I set aside time every week to call clients and see if they're still happy in their homes?

6. Do I make a habit of asking for referrals?

7. If I say I'm going to call someone back, do I do it as soon as I can?

8. If I promise to send out some information, is it in the mail that day? Do I call a day or two later to see if they have any questions?

9. Do I have records so I can keep track of my performance? Do I evaluate myself at the end of every day, month, and year?

Do all of the above and you're well on your way to successful farming. Ignore any of them, and watch out.

Final Thoughts

Don't expect miracles overnight. Just as with agricultural farming, real estate farming takes time. Moreover, whether you farm extensively by phone, by mail, or in person, successful farming is a long series of small steps which make the big ones possible.

Thousands of real estate professionals nationwide have proved the success of farming — and you can, too. Good luck.

Recommended Reading

How to Increase Sales and Put Yourself Across by Telephone by Mona Ling (Prentice Hall, 1963)

Reach Out & Sell Someone by Dr. Gary S. Goodman (Prentice Hall, 1983)

Successful Telemarketing by Bob Stone & John Wyman (NTC Business Books, 1986)

Successful Telephone Selling in the '80s by Martin D. Shafiroff and Robert L. Shook (Barnes and Noble Books, 1982)

Telephone Techniques That Sell by Charles Bury (Warner Books 1980)

You Can Sell Anything by Telephoning by Dr. Gary S. Goodman (Prentice Hall, 1984)

How I Raised Myself from Failure to Success in Selling by Frank Bettger (Prentice Hall, 1947)

How to Master the Art of Selling by Tom Hopkins (Warner Books, 1982)

How to Sell Anything to Anybody by Joe Girard (Warner Books, 1977)

Zig Ziglar's Secrets of Closing the Sale by Zig Ziglar (Berkley Books, 1984)

INDEX

Also Available from Calculated Industries

Financial I™ Real Estate Calculator

The world's simplest calculator for real estate. Figures everything from payments to interest rates to yields on investments and much, much more — all with the touch of a few buttons. Also works as a regular math calculator with percent, memory and auto shut-off. Includes case, instructions, 1-year warranty, and long-life batteries. (Measures 2-3/4 x 5-1/4 x 1/4") Only $29.95 (plus $3.50 shpg.).

Conventional-Plus and *FHA/VA Qualifiers*™

New easy-to-use slide charts let you qualify your prospects in seconds, showing you what price range and what loan programs best suit your clients. Handle regular VA and VA-GPM, FHA 203-B and 245-Plan III, and 15- and 30-Year Conventional. Conv.-Plus Qualifier™ *or FHA/VA Qualifier*™ *$6.50 ea. (plus $1.50 shpg.) or order both together for $11.95 (plus $2.50 shpg.).*

Ranging 100™ *Optical TapeMeasure*®

Measure how far, how high, or how wide with the Ranging 100™ *Optical TapeMeasure*®*. Just look through it like a camera, focus and read your measurement. Ranges 6 feet to 100 feet. Pocket-sized and rugged, comes with 2-year warranty and full instructions. Only $39.95 (plus $3.50 shpg.) — optional padded case, $6.50.*

For more information, or to order, write to:

Calculated Industries, Inc.

2010 N. Tustin Avenue • Orange • CA • 92665

Notes